A BURST OF SUNSHINE AFTER RAIN AT HUNTLEY POND

AFTERNOON OF A GRAY OCTOBER DAY AT INDIAN PASS

A SUN-SPECKLED FOREST NEAR THE HUDSON GORGE

WINTER LIGHT ON UPPER CASCADE LAKE

A MEADOW IN SUMMER NEAR MORIAH

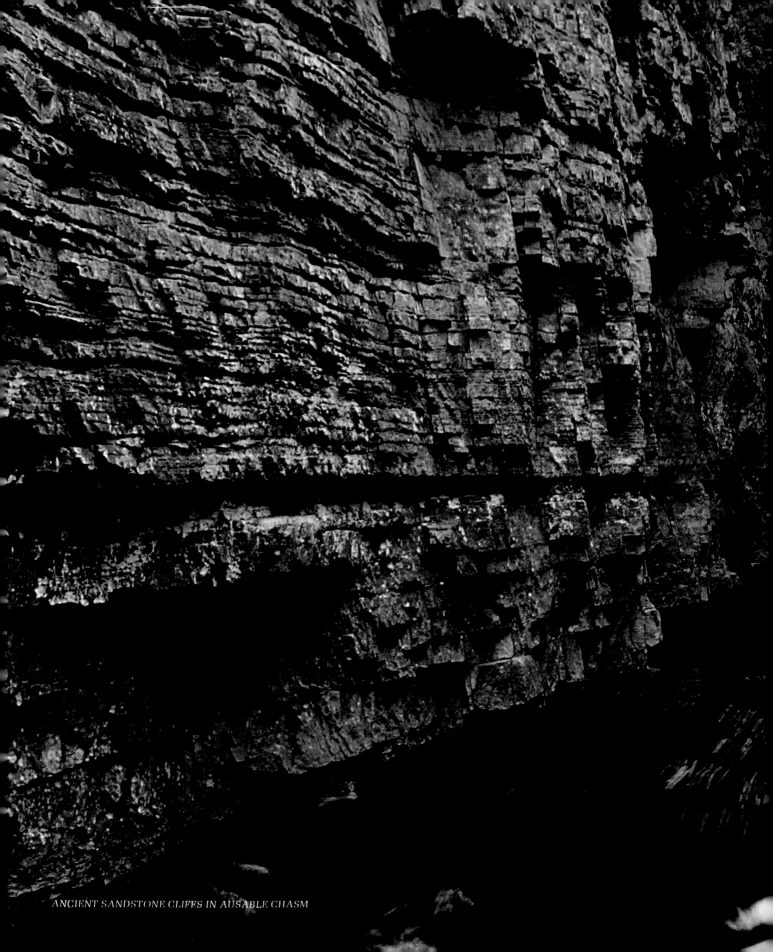
ANCIENT SANDSTONE CLIFFS IN AUSABLE CHASM

SNOW-DUSTED HILLSIDES AT LOWER AUSABLE LAKE

THE ANCIENT ADIRONDACKS

THE AMERICAN WILDERNESS/TIME-LIFE BOOKS/NEW YORK

BY LINCOLN BARNETT
AND THE EDITORS OF TIME-LIFE BOOKS

TIME-LIFE BOOKS

FOUNDER: Henry R. Luce 1898-1967

Editor-in-Chief: Hedley Donovan
Chairman of the Board: Andrew Heiskell
President: James R. Shepley
Chairman, Executive Committee: James A. Linen
Group Vice President: Rhett Austell

Vice Chairman: Roy E. Larsen

MANAGING EDITOR: Jerry Korn
Assistant Managing Editors: David Maness,
Martin Mann, A. B. C. Whipple
Planning Director: Oliver E. Allen
Art Director: Sheldon Cotler
Chief of Research: Beatrice T. Dobie
Director of Photography: Melvin L. Scott
Senior Text Editor: Diana Hirsh
Assistant Art Director: Arnold C. Holeywell

PUBLISHER: Joan D. Manley
General Manager: John D. McSweeney
Business Manager: John Steven Maxwell
Sales Director: Carl G. Jaeger
Promotion Director: Paul R. Stewart
Public Relations Director: Nicholas Benton

THE AMERICAN WILDERNESS

SERIES EDITOR: Charles Osborne
Editorial Staff for *The Ancient Adirondacks:*
Text Editor: Jay Brennan
Picture Editor: Patricia Hunt
Designer: Charles Mikolaycak
Staff Writers: Simone D. Gossner, Sam Halper,
Susan Hillaby
Chief Researcher: Martha T. Goolrick
Researchers: Muriel Clarke, Terry Drucker,
Barbara Ensrud, Villette Harris,
Beatrice Hsia, Suzanne Wittebort
Design Assistant: Vincent Lewis

Editorial Production
Production Editor: Douglas B. Graham
Assistant: Gennaro C. Esposito
Quality Director: Robert L. Young
Assistant: James J. Cox
Copy Staff: Rosalind Stubenberg (chief),
Barbara Quarmby, Mary Ellen Slate,
Florence Keith
Picture Department: Dolores A. Littles,
Joan Lynch

Valuable assistance in the preparation of this
book was given by the following departments
and individuals of Time Inc.: Editorial
Production, Norman Airey; Library, Benjamin
Lightman; Picture Collection, Doris O'Neil;
Photographic Laboratory, George Karas; TIME-
LIFE News Service, Murray J. Gart.

The Author: Lincoln Barnett has been a staff writer, war correspondent and editor for LIFE magazine, and the author of several volumes for Time Inc., including *The World We Live In* and *The Wonders of Life on Earth.* He also wrote *The Universe and Dr. Einstein, The Treasure of Our Tongue* and *Writing on Life.* A lover of the Adirondacks since boyhood, he lives in Westport, New York, on Lake Champlain.

The Cover: Paper-birch trees near the summit of Mount Noonmark bend to the winds of an oncoming autumnal storm. The frontal clouds of the storm, which has enveloped Baxter Mountain in the center background, cast dark shadows on Keene Valley as they sweep eastward to the slopes of Spread Eagle Mountain at right.

Contents

1/ The Green Mosaic 20

Fountainhead of a New Art 36

2/ The Inland Sea 44

A Walk on Haystack Mountain 58

3/ The High Peaks 70

Secret Sources of the Hudson 86

4/ The Deep Woods 102

Prelude to Winter 116

5/ The Bounteous Waters 126

An Obdurate Mountain Passage 140

6/ The Great Pass 152

The Ponds of Autumn 166

Bibliography 180

Acknowledgments and Credits 181

Index 182

The Biggest Wild Park in the States

Dominating the northeast sector of New York state (tinted rectangle above), the Adirondack wilderness contains the largest park in the United States. Lying within the area shown in green at right, the six-million-acre Adirondack State Park (roughly the size of neighboring Vermont) is bounded by the so-called Blue Line, which is also shown here in red to avoid confusion with watercourses. The park includes the headwaters of the Hudson and 100-odd miles of its course. Yet this stretch represents less than 1 per cent of the region's flowing waters, many of which arise among the park's 27 major peaks.

More than one third of the park is administered by the State of New York as the Adirondack Forest Preserve (areas of darker green on the map). Throughout, the parkland, a complex amalgam of public and private lands, is densely wooded with conifers and hardwoods, and dotted by uncounted lakes and ponds. Most wild areas may be reached over trails (those mentioned in the text are shown as black lines) maintained by New York state and by such private organizations as the Adirondack Mountain Club.

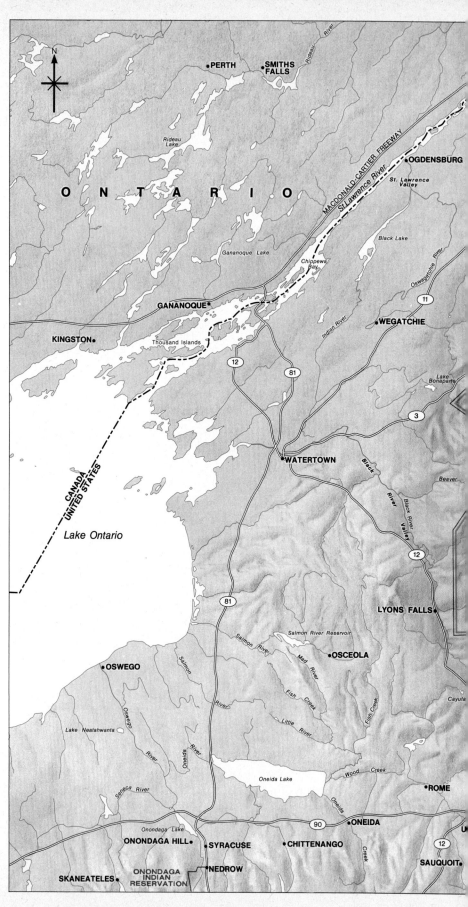

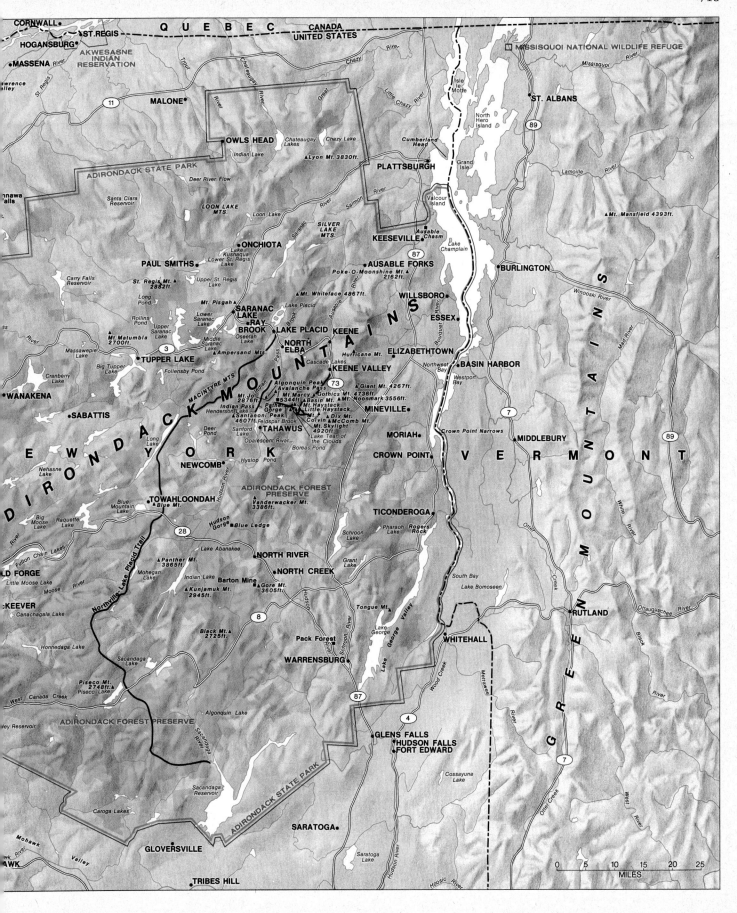

1/ The Green Mosaic

We gaze downward from the mountain...upon thousands of square miles of wilderness, which...hides the secrets of form, and soil, and rock, and history, on which we ponder.   VERPLANCK COLVIN/ *REPORT TO THE NEW YORK LEGISLATURE*

One red and gold September morning, in the company of a few friends, I started up Mount Noonmark, my favorite peak in the whole Adirondack wilderness. It is not one of the so-called High Peaks—a category reserved for the 46 mountains approaching or exceeding 4,000 feet in altitude—but in an ascent to its bare and precipitous summit, 3,556 feet high, one traverses almost every form of terrain and forest zone, and sees almost every variety of tree and montane plant observable on the major mountains of the main range.

I have climbed Noonmark perhaps half a hundred times since my affair with it began at the age of 14, and my passion for the 360° view from the top has never abated. Northward you can see the whole main range of the Adirondacks, from Marcy and Haystack in the western distance, through the whole sweep of the central peaks down to Noonmark's neighbor, Giant Mountain, bastion of the eastern slopes. To the south, the huge massif of the Dix range bursts upon you only after you surmount the last breathless rocky pitch at the climax of the demanding Stimson Trail—named for Henry L. Stimson, former Secretary of State and Secretary of War, who pioneered the route half a century ago. These splendors can be attained in a climb of less than two hours from the road below on the Ausable Club preserve.

On this special day the weather was made for climbing: cool and tranquil amid the green shadows of the giant hemlock, beech and yellow-birch groves at the foot of Noonmark and brisk and breezy on the upper slopes. I can think of no more dramatic moment in Adirondack climbing than that which occurs when, after some 45 minutes of steep ascent through the lower and middle forest zones, the Stimson Trail suddenly levels off, skirts a small cliff, then leaps sharply upward; it leads you, scrambling for toeholds and handholds, to a dazzling promontory, a charmed magic casement opening on the ramparts of the main range, the long corridor of Keene Valley and, far away to the north, the symmetrical pyramid of Whiteface, solitary sentinel of Lake Placid, fifth-highest peak in the Adirondacks, aloof and austere.

It is at this first stunning exposure, when you pause to breathe and wonder, that you recall how Noonmark got its name: down in the village of Keene Valley, three miles to the north, one sees the sun directly above the peak of the mountain at high noon.

From this not-quite-halfway point, we continued upward through elfin evergreen, stunted silver birch and poplar thickets, all overlying the thin soil cover of the billion-year-old Adirondack uplift. The summit recurrently glowered above us, a forbidding citadel, much more hostile seen from below than on top, though no ropes or pitons or special equipment are needed to scale its ultimate heights. Tennis shoes will do, but many faint hearts have surrendered at these first perspectives. Overhead, at the zenith, the sky shone a deep-sea blue.

At one of the many slanting ledges on the open shoulder we met a group of descending hikers—a young husband and wife, one small boy, one baby in a pack basket on the husband's back and one beamish beagle. We paused to chat in the fraternal fashion of all Adirondackers.

"Many people on top?" "Quite a few, I think four parties, maybe 20 altogether." "Oh God! Crowded! Population explosion!" "Well, you know, this time of year, and a great day."

We all gazed up the valley. On a clear day, from the summit of Noonmark, the range of vision may extend nearly a hundred miles, wherever it is not blocked by higher mountains—eastward across Lake Champlain to the Green Mountains of Vermont, southward to Schroon Lake and the upper reaches of the Hudson River where it emerges, tamed, from its wild gorges and curves gently down to Glens Falls and Albany. Yet on this cloudless noon a hazy scrim blurred the distant vistas.

"Quite a bit of autumn haze," I said.

"That's not autumn haze," my new friend said, shifting his pack as the baby began to protest the delay. "It's smog."

"Smog! From where? We're miles . . ."

"Well, you know weather generally moves from west to east. The smog comes from industrial cities to the west—Syracuse, Rochester, Buffalo. Some of it may even come from Cleveland, Detroit or Chicago. Well, enjoy your climb. You may never have a better day."

Noonmark rises amid the High Peaks area in the northeast quadrant of the Adirondacks, the wildest and most spectacular region of New York state, where the land falls away abruptly in the 40 miles from the 5,344-foot summit of Mount Marcy, highest of all the peaks, to the shores of Lake Champlain, a mere 100 feet above sea level.

When people speak of the Adirondacks, what do they envisage? Mountains? Forests? Lake country? It is all of these. The Adirondack Park, covering some 9,475 square miles, comprises a green and blue mosaic of ancient mountains, among the oldest in the country; more than 1,345 lakes with names (and hundreds without names); and millions of acres of hardwood and evergreen forest, the whole iridescent tapestry cross-stitched by roads and embroidered with small hamlets, villages and towns. It is bounded on the north by the Saint Lawrence River, on the east by Lake Champlain, on the south by the Mohawk River; on the west it extends along the Black River nearly to Lake Ontario. Within these confines the Adirondack pageant of lakes and woods and mountains is infinitely variegated, creased by deep ravines and gorges, striated by streams and rushing brooks, ribboned with cascades and waterfalls, and aglitter with thousands of acres of bird-haunted wetlands.

It might be said that the Adirondacks are divided into four parts. To mountain climbers, the name Adirondacks means the High Peaks area in the wild northeastern quadrant, embossed with five ranges running generally parallel to each other from northeast to southwest, separated by valleys and lakes, linked here and there by subsidiary ribs and ridges. To boatmen and fishermen, who come in numbers from Utica and Syracuse, the Adirondacks connote the lake and river country amid the forest canopy that mantles the low hills cradling the Fulton Chain in the more populous southwest quadrant. To weekenders from Albany and Troy, the Adirondacks are symbolized by Schroon Lake and Lake George in the equally populous southeast quadrant. And to residents of the Saint Lawrence Valley, both American and Canadian, the Adirondacks are the relatively flat and empty spaces of the northwest quadrant —the Saint Regis River, the Raquette River and Cranberry Lake.

But these connotations are subjective, not official or political concepts. To understand the Adirondacks, it is necessary first to distinguish between the Adirondack Mountains, the Adirondack Forest Preserve and the Adirondack Park. The panorama is blurred by a concatenation of geology, history, politics and paradox. The primary paradox is that this wilderness lies close to the most densely populated section of the United States—scarcely 200 miles north of New York City. Yet a great part of it was virtually unknown, save to parties of warring Indians, Frenchmen, Englishmen and Americans until the 1830s. The headwaters of the Columbia River in the Far West were discovered more than a half century before the highest headwaters of the Hudson. Stanley had found Livingston in darkest Africa before most New Yorkers knew much about the wilderness at their back door.

The very name Adirondacks was not applied to the area until 1838, when Ebenezer Emmons, a professor and chief geologist of the first state topographical survey of the region, wrote in his report: "The cluster of mountains in the neighborhood of the Upper Hudson and Ausable rivers I propose to call the *Adirondack Group,* a name by which a well known tribe of Indians who once hunted here may be commemorated." The linguistic origin of the name has been discussed and debated by historians and etymologists for years. One traditional view is that it may have been a pejorative Iroquois term for the Algonquins, traditional enemies of the Iroquois from Canada, who supposedly were forced to live on tree buds and bark during the harsh winter months; the Iroquoian epithet *ratirontaks,* meaning "those who eat trees," implied that the Algonquins were improvident in summer and autumn and too weak to hunt in winter. Some linguists have suggested different lines of descent. One point, however, is clear: there was an Algonquin tribe known as the Adirondacks based in the Montreal area. Whether the tribe actually hunted in the Adirondacks can never be known for certain.

There are no such semantic complexities in differentiating between the Adirondack Park and the Adironack Forest Preserve. The Adirondack Park embraces the entire six-million-acre area, including both state-owned and privately owned land, that falls within the so-called Blue Line—a symbol used on official New York state maps to define the boundaries of the park when it was first created three quarters of a century ago. The state-owned land is known as the Adirondack Forest Preserve. Let us look first at the park. To begin with, it can lay claim to a superlative that may surprise some Westerners in particular: *The Adirondack Park is the biggest park, state or national, in the United States.* Its total area is two and a half times that of Yellowstone—in fact, greater than the combined areas of Yellowstone, Yosemite, Grand Canyon,

Glacier and Olympic national parks (which total about 5.5 million acres). It is larger than Connecticut, larger than New Jersey. To provide a closer analogy, the Adirondack Park is about the size of Vermont.

Of the total park area of six million acres, more than a third is owned by the state and protected by Article XIV of the New York State Constitution, ratified in 1894, which decreed that the Adirondack Forest Preserve cannot "be leased, sold or exchanged . . . nor shall the timber thereon be sold, removed or destroyed. . . ." and, most memorably, that "the forest preserve . . . shall be forever kept as wild forest lands." This article has become famous as the "Forever Wild" provision. It was fought from the outset by land speculators, lumbermen and mining companies, and it is still the focus of conflict between those who hold that "locking up" the forests is a barrier to progress and those who believe that preserving the wilderness is an ecological and sociological necessity. Since 1895, of more than 125 proposals introduced in the legislature to weaken Article XIV, only 16 have been approved at the polls. By and large, therefore, the citizens of New York state have helped to maintain the forest preserve not only for esthetic and recreational reasons, but as the sanctuary of a vital watershed.

At the moment the sanctity of the forest preserve seems assured, though its tracts are not all contiguous but scattered in crazy-quilt fashion about the park in parcels ranging in size from less than 10 to 300,000 acres. But what of the other 3.7 million acres of privately held land? The Blue Line has been revised and extended repeatedly to encompass newly acquired lands. It was first drawn in the hope that the area it delineated would eventually become a solid and homogeneous state-owned entity. That hope flickered and failed; today the Adirondack Park is a jigsaw puzzle, with public and private woodlands flourishing indiscriminately side by side. So in one sense, the Blue Line is somewhat of an anachronism. Yet every consideration of the future of the Adirondacks involves what is inside the Blue Line—a jagged rectangle roughly 120 miles on each eccentric side. It staggers up the middle of Lake Champlain, including New York's half of the lake in the park, thrusts north and west past Chazy and Chateaugay lakes almost to the Canadian border, pushes westward past the extreme fringes of the forest to the gentle meadowlands of the Black River plain, then swoops south through the Hinckley Reservoir and back east again to encompass the huge expanse of Great Sacandaga Lake.

As of today the 3.7 million acres of private land within the Blue Line

Lake Placid, sheltered from the wind by nearby hills and the bulk of Whiteface Mountain (rear), exhales mist early in an autumn evening.

are botanically virtually identical with the state-owned forests, owing in part to complementary relationships between the larger landowners and the New York State Department of Environmental Conservation. Almost 80 per cent of this private land is devoted to open-space uses (e.g., hiking, camping, canoeing) and cannot be distinguished by air or by land from the preserves. The biggest landowners are paper companies—the International Paper Company, the St. Regis Paper Company and Finch, Pruyn & Company. Each of these corporate giants owns more than 125,000 acres of Adirondack forest land. Although the operations of their pulp mills, all but one of which are outside the park, occasionally pollute the air in the park when the wind blows toward it, the companies are as deeply concerned as the state ecologists with the fragility and future of the woodlands on which their profits depend.

Next down the scale of private landowners come 32 corporations and individuals that hold more than 10,000 acres each and collectively own 1,171,390 acres. All in all, within the private-land category, there are 626 owners whose individual holdings exceed 500 acres and who together own nearly two million acres—53 per cent of the private lands within the Blue Line.

It was with such facts in mind that in September 1968 Governor Nelson Rockefeller appointed a Temporary Study Commission on the Future of the Adirondacks. Some two years later, the commission's massive report reached the Governor's desk. Most notably, it recommended the creation of an independent, bipartisan Adirondack Park Agency authorized to prepare master plans for the future use of both state-owned and private lands, and empowered to regulate such use.

"If the Adirondacks are to be saved, time is of the essence," wrote Harold K. Hochschild, founder of the Adirondack Museum at Blue Mountain Lake and chairman of the commission. His sense of urgency derived from many portents: moves by out-of-state developers to buy up huge tracts of land and erect grandiose second-home communities within the park area; the absence of any zoning regulations in more than 90 per cent of the private land within the park; and the seasonal explosion of the park's population from 125,000 year-round residents to a summer high of more than nine million transients.

Following a bruising battle in the state legislature, the agency was born toward the end of 1971. Within the next two years, after intensive study and many acrimonious public hearings, the agency produced two master plans, one for the state lands, one for the private lands. The first of these, released in June 1972, divided the state lands into five major categories: Wilderness Areas, Primitive Areas, Canoe Areas, Wild Forest Areas and Intensive Use Areas.

The Wilderness Areas, totaling nearly a million acres, included those places "where the earth and its community of life are untrammeled by man—where man himself is a visitor who does not remain." Here all nonconforming entities such as roads, snowmobile and jeep trails, tent platforms and boat docks, must be phased out by 1975; access must be by foot or horseback; no motorized vehicles or aircraft will be allowed except in emergencies. Primitive Areas, the next category, were defined as essentially wilderness in character, but for one reason or another—the existence of a necessary road or, as in the case of Valcour Island in Lake Champlain, a lighthouse—could not be awarded the Wilderness classification. Canoe Areas were to be managed under Wilderness guidelines—no motorboats, no motor access. In Wild Forest Areas—encompassing nearly 1.2 million acres, or 52 per cent of the forest preserve—a wider range of regulated recreational activities, such as limited snowmobiling, were to be permitted. The remaining public lands, classified as Intensive Use Areas, were those that already had campgrounds, ski centers, public beaches and boat-launching sites.

Inasmuch as the State Land Master Plan did not require the approval of the legislature, Governor Rockefeller simply announced in July 1972 that it had become state policy for the management of its preserves in the Adirondack Park. But the agency's Land Use and Development Plan —specifying controls on private land, zoning, population density, lake frontages, billboards and all forms of pollution—was another matter. It did require legislative approval, and upon its release in 1972, fireworks exploded throughout upstate New York and, most violently, in Albany. Under this plan, all private lands in the Adirondack Park were to be divided into six categories—hamlets, moderate-intensity use, low-intensity use, rural use, resource-management use (particularly of forest and agricultural resources), industrial use—with guidelines regulating the development of each. The legislature, after another ferocious session of infighting, finally passed the plan in 1973.

It was when I first inspected the agency's official park map, which limns the various categories of land use in different shades of green, that I realized the Adirondacks are indeed a green mosaic, both on paper and in fact. And I realized something else: that in all my years as an Adirondacker, I had never explored in depth the fastnesses of the park beyond the northeast quadrant where I live. With this thought in mind, I dropped in one day at agency headquarters in Ray Brook, near the village of Saranac Lake. There I talked with George D. Davis, assistant director of the agency.

"The best way to get a feeling for the whole park," he said, "is to fly across the area, around the Blue Line, with sorties into the interior. It will give you a sense of the amazing variety of land forms in the Adirondacks. Other parks and other wilderness areas in the country have bigger mountains, bigger rivers, bigger lakes, but practically nowhere else are they all brought together as strikingly as they are here.

"I should warn you that you'll detect some scars, scars the agency can do nothing about," George continued. "At Tahawus, for example, you'll see a great open-strip titanium mine, the biggest in the world. But most of these scars are out of the past, part of history, and in our lifetime at least, they are probably irreversible."

George added that he hoped he would be able to go along on the flight. My pilot would be Clarence Petty, a born-and-bred Adirondacker, and the closest facsimile of an omniscient bush pilot that one can find in the region. He is not only a skilled flier but a forestry expert on the staff of the Adirondack Park Agency; he requires no maps and can instantly identify every lake, pond, mountain and low hill, and inform you of its history, geology, flora and fauna. Our other companion on the flight would be the agency's chief biologist, Greenleaf Chase, a slender, soft-spoken gentleman whose name, I thought, was almost astrologically ordained for a biologist and outdoorsman.

As it turned out, George was not free when the right day dawned after an interval of rain, overcast and ground fog. But Clarence and Greenie were there at the Lake Placid Airport at 10 o'clock on a sunny September morning. We decided to fly counterclockwise from Lake Placid, which is a bit northeast of the center of the park, and head northwest over the lake country I had only infrequently seen. We spiraled upward, with the mile-high façade of Mount Whiteface, etched with ski trails and its motor road, towering to the north, and below us the village of Lake Placid, which stands not on Lake Placid but on Mirror Lake. Lake Placid itself lies to the west. Although I knew many houses lined its shores, they lay hidden in the needled woods. There was no turbulence as we flew smoothly westward, the big mountains behind us, the rolling lake country before us.

"On your right," Clarence said, "are the Saranac Lakes—Upper, Middle and Lower, reading from left to right."

We were at about 6,000 feet and no signs of human existence could be discerned, save for a few white plumes of water to indicate that some small motorboats had ruffled the blue surface of the lakes.

"One of the best outlooks in the Adirondacks," Clarence went on, "is from Ampersand Mountain, there on the south shore of Middle Saranac Lake, with the fire tower on top. It's an easy climb and gives you a view not only of the Saranac Lakes, but of the main range to the south." I reflected momentarily on the oddity of Ampersand as a name for a mountain. As in most such matters in the Adirondacks there are at least two theories of its derivation. One is that espoused by Verplanck Colvin, the great topographical surveyor of the Adirondacks for nearly four decades from 1865 to 1900, who had remarked on the "amber sands" embracing the Saranac Lakes and islands and attributed the name to the sands. The other derivation was suggested by Henry Van Dyke of Princeton, who in 1885 conjectured that the mountain had received its name from a small meandering stream emanating from a lake behind it. "It is such a crooked stream," he wrote, "so bent and curved and twisted upon itself, so fond of turning around . . . corners and sweeping away in great circles from its direct course, that its first explorers christened it after the eccentric supernumerary of the alphabet which appears in the old spelling books as &."

Now we saw beneath us a variegated carpet of treetops, full and opulent in the richness of summer, interwoven with the darker spires of conifers. Off to our right, the north, we saw the Saint Regis Lakes, looking like the lapis-lazuli pieces of a fragmented Chinese puzzle.

We flew over Saint Regis Mountain, surmounted by a fire warden's tower. "They'll probably take that tower down," Clarence continued. "The park agency feels that towers impair the wilderness aspect, and that fire patrols can be conducted more efficiently by plane and at a lower cost than by keeping fire wardens in seasonal residence.

"Take a look at this whole Saint Regis area, the lakes and ponds —canoe country. You can make a loop of 25 to 30 miles by canoe. The longest carry is about one mile from Long Pond to Bessie Pond. And down there toward Tupper Lake Village are the two largest state-owned campsites in the Adirondack Park, on Fish Creek and Rollins Pond."

I could see some cabin roofs and small docks and boats as Clarence banked for my benefit. I also noted some yellow, weedy ponds and asked him if they were victims of man-made waste.

Greenie Chase, who was sitting behind us, heard my question. "Bogs and bog ponds are natural and quite unique ecological features of the

From the summit of Mount Noonmark
the Adirondack landscape sweeps
for miles toward the Dix range,
easternmost rampart of the High Peaks
area. The top of Dix Mountain
shows at far right; next to it—partially
hidden—is Hough Peak. From there the
range slopes down toward McComb
Mountain, with its rockslide scar, and
melts into the eastern foothills.

park. All plants flower, but in some bogs the presence of calcium permits greater aquatic plant variety and degree of flowering.''

"The Tupper Lake marshes, by the way, are good duck-hunting country," said Clarence.

Off to our left, we saw Long Lake, a sapphire bracelet 13 miles long, though at some places only a hundred yards wide. "See the ledges on that mountain over there?" said Greenie Chase. "It's eagle territory. But please don't mention the name of the mountain. There are a lot of egg collectors around, and as you know, the bald eagle and the golden eagle are vanishing species in the Adirondacks, barely hanging on the thread of the environment. The golden eagle is basically a Western bird, an open-land hunter. It moved here after the Adirondack woods were burned off in a couple of devastating forest fires in 1903 and 1908. But now that the forests are beginning to close in again, the golden eagle is on the way out as a species. As for the bald eagle, he migrates in winter to shallow, estuarine waters where he is subject to pollution and pesticides. So one thing the eagles don't need is harassment from egg collectors. I've climbed those ledges over there many times looking up and seeing eagles. Today I've been looking down instead of up, and I'm sad to say I haven't seen an eagle yet."

We continued southwestward, through still air, past Long Lake, then Blue Mountain Lake with its spangled islands and superbly sculptured mountain at the northeastern end. We flew on over the green forest canopy to the blue imprint of Raquette Lake (*raquette* is the French word for snowshoe). It was on the shores of this lake that there arose in the latter part of the 19th Century the original design of the famous "Adirondack camp"—a merger of the early Adirondack log cabin with decorative features of the Swiss chalet, including gables, balconies and porches, all blending into the forest and lakeshore setting.

In the distance we could now discern the Fulton Chain Lakes, strung out like beads on a necklace, unimaginatively numbered from one to eight, and unimaginatively built up, cottage to cottage, dock to dock. "We're just about at the western perimeter of the Blue Line," Clarence said. "That's the Black River plain ahead." And as he pointed, I noticed that the forests were thinning out. In the distance there glowed a green and yellow Cézanne landscape of meadowlands.

We banked now to the left, changing our course to the south and east, passing over dozens of lakes with eminently forgettable names like Round Pond and Long Pond. Much of the nomenclature of the Adirondacks is uninspired. There are, it is true, some place names of haunting and evocative resonance, like Lake Tear of the Clouds, the Opalescent River, Pharaoh Lake, Mount Skylight, Poke-O-Moonshine Mountain. But the highest peak in the main range, Marcy, was named for a public official, and as far as water bodies are concerned, there are no less than 20 Long Ponds, 10 East Ponds, 16 Clear Ponds, 20 Mud Ponds, 10 Round Ponds, 10 Duck Ponds, 12 Otter Ponds—and no one can define the difference between a pond and a lake. A friend of mine owns a lovely lake, a mile long, half a mile wide, which until recently was called Warm Pond—one of countless Warm Ponds in the Adirondacks, many of them quite cold. My friend decided that his beautiful lake deserved a better name. Historical research revealed that at one time an old forge had stood beside this highland lake. So he petitioned the state for permission to rename his pond. Warm Pond, I am happy to say, is now Highlands Forge Lake.

"Look down at that spruce swamp along the Moose River," Clarence said as we flew on, a little bumpily now, to the southeast. "That's one of the main wintering grounds of the Adirondack deer. You know that in winter, exposure from lack of shelter forces the deer out of high places. They suffer from cold just as we do, and seek refuge in evergreen borders beside rivers. Deer winter here because of the spruce, fir and other conifers that grow along the drainage. Basically it's shelter, not food, that determines a deer's choice of wintering area—though the amount of food available in a severe winter can be critical."

Ahead of us now I could see two large bodies of water—one was Piseco Lake, the other the great man-made lake, Sacandaga Reservoir. We were beginning to bounce around a bit as we encountered thermals warmed by the noonday sun. Overhead and sometimes right off our wingtips gauzy patches of summer cumulus drifted by and shook us genially in passing.

Flying over the reservoir, we shifted course again, this time to the northeast, and in the distance saw pillars of sulfurous smoke rising from the Finch, Pruyn pulp and paper mill at Glens Falls, outside the Blue Line. It was just about noon, and Clarence said, "Well, we're halfway around the line. Shall we go up through Lake George and Lake Champlain into the northeast quadrant?"

I said, "I've flown over Lake George and Lake Champlain and I know how beautiful they are. I'd rather go up the Hudson River to Lake Tear of the Clouds and see that from the air. I've never seen the Hudson Gorge, the Blue Ledge and the wild, white-water part of the Hudson."

We took a turn above the Hudson at Glens Falls, and noticed how the color of the water changed as it left the sanctuary of the Blue Line. Upstream from the paper mill the water was dark and clear. Below the mill it was yellow sludge. We veered northward, passed over the town of Warrensburg, and I observed that at this point the Hudson was flowing, perhaps 75 yards wide, tranquil, wandering among green meadows, cradled by small comforting hills. Then, a few miles above Warrensburg, the rapids began.

"This is where they hold the white-water races," Clarence said. "Most people think of the Colorado River or the Snake River as places to shoot rapids. These can be just as exciting, and just as dangerous."

As we continued north the thin line of the Hudson River became still narrower and increasingly dappled with white rapids that looked like whipped cream from 5,000 feet. A mountain loomed to the west.

"Gore Mountain, North Creek," Clarence said. "Popular ski area on this side. But let me show you the back." He banked, swung around, and there on the northwest slope we saw one of the major scars of the Adirondack Park. "This," Clarence said, "is the Barton Mine, largest garnet mine in the world. The Barton Mines Corporation has operated open-pit mines here for years. So you can't really complain too much about the ski area on the east side of Gore as a park defacement."

Upstream from the mountain, the Hudson continued to look thinner and whiter, and the rapids more forbidding. And then we came to the main gorge and caught a glimpse of the walled canyon that rose some 500 feet above the water and at the dense forest that crested it like an Indian headdress. Clarence dipped his wing and pointed to a waterfall.

"That's known as the O.K. Slip Waterfall," he said. "It's about 250 feet high, the highest waterfall in the Adirondacks. It gets its name from a lumberman's term. It simply meant that the loggers regarded the area just below the waterfall as an O.K. place to slide their timber down to the river."

A mile or so farther upstream we spotted Blue Ledge, a 300-foot-high granitic cliff almost hidden among the forest gallery flanking the river; it reflected blue on blue in a deep-water pool of infinite calm at its base.

"This is the best way to see the Blue Ledge," Clarence said, executing a 360° turn to linger over the scene. "It's a fair bushwhack in from the nearest road. And if you decide to do it by some kind of boat —well, once you start down there's no turning back, no way out."

As we continued north the Hudson shrank to a silver thread. Ahead loomed the great south face of Mount Marcy, and at its feet the unbelievable scar of the titanium mine, a gaping, gray crater nearly a mile in diameter. It looked like the gateway to hell.

I averted my eyes from the unpleasant sight and looked away to the High Peaks. The spider strand of the Hudson now disappeared behind forested slopes as we climbed the thin air over Marcy. But I knew that at about this point it met the Opalescent River, its east tributary, and then Feldspar Brook, which trickles down from Lake Tear of the Clouds. Then the teardrop of the lake itself appeared, caught fleetingly in its rocky vial 900 feet below the summit of Marcy, 4,400 feet above the sea where its virgin waters would someday arrive.

As we soared above the mile-high dome of Marcy, we saw some hikers on top, lunching in the afternoon sun.

"Quite a few people on top today," I said.

"I bet they're not happy about us flying over them," Greenie replied.

We continued north to the last segment of the Blue Line, whence we saw the Saint Lawrence spread out as a hazy band of pale silver in the afternoon light. We flew over the village of Owls Head, which year after year reports the lowest temperature readings in the state. "That's just because of some energetic newspaper stringer," Greenie observed. "Actually the coldest readings on record have come from the State Ranger School at Wanakena. They've had frost pockets of 60 below."

As we turned south again just west of the Lake Champlain Valley, I said I wanted to make one more pass over the main range, from Giant to Gothics to Haystack to Marcy to Algonquin.

"Okay," Clarence said. So once again I looked down on the craggy mountains I had climbed so often and felt somewhat guilty at seeing them from an airplane, with no expenditure of muscular effort or shortness of breath.

As we dropped down from the heights into the small field at Lake Placid, Clarence remarked casually, "You know, I hardly ever used to fly a plane with wheels on a flight like this."

"Why?"

"Well, you saw all those lakes and ponds. There aren't many places you can land on wheels in these mountains if you get in trouble. In a floatplane you can set down anywhere."

Fountainhead of a New Art

From the moment the Adirondacks were first named, their deep, silent forests, tumbling streams and waterfalls, still lakes and soaring mountains inspired artists. The report of the scientific survey of 1837 suggesting the name "Adirondacks" was illustrated with lithographs based on the work of a fashionable New York portraitist, Charles Cromwell Ingham (1796-1863), who had joined the expedition to make sketches.

But Ingham was more than just an observer. He was one of a group of individualistic and romantic painters who arrived on the Adirondack scene at a time when the wilderness was first coming to be regarded as more than an obstacle in the path of material progress. These artists were quick to discover a profound sense of mystery and wonder in the presence of the region's beauty, and they saw a golden chance to capture its untamed quality on canvas.

Paradoxically, Thomas Cole, the leader of the first truly American school of landscape art, was English-born. In his passion for the New World, Cole uprooted his whole family to America in 1819. Wandering the upper reaches of the Hudson River, Cole would play his flute, make a few sketches, and then retire to his studio to complete the luminous works that, as an admirer said at his funeral in 1848, "carried the eye over scenes of wild grandeur peculiar to our country, over our aerial mountain tops with their mighty growth of forest never touched by the axe, along the banks of streams never deformed by culture."

Another immigrant was the dashing French landscapist Régis Gignoux (1816-1882), who followed a young woman to America, married her and then fell in love with the wilderness of New York state.

Most of the painters, however, were native-born, though from different backgrounds. Samuel Colman (1832-1920), whose father was a fine-arts book publisher, worked out of a sumptuous New York City studio apartment. The moody Alexander Helwig Wyant (1836-1892), once a saddle-maker's apprentice, preferred a house in the Adirondacks, where he spent the summers between 1874 and 1880 distilling his impressions of rocks, brooks and woods.

Whatever the background or personality of the individual artist, they were all united by a love of the Adirondacks, and their work helped start the movement to keep America's wildernesses "forever wild."

Though Alexander Helwig Wyant's painting The Flume, Opalescent River shows the broad, bold, almost impressionistic technique he used after a stroke forced him to change to his left hand, it is still faithful in its details: the water has the characteristic brown color of many Adirondack streams, caused by iron in the rocks and acids from decomposing leaves and bark.

In Samuel Colman's Au Sable River, a
trout fisherman is dwarfed by boulders
tumbled in a river still well known
for the excellence of its fishing. An
early art critic, struck by Colman's use
of color, wrote that it had "a
brilliance that is so harmonious as to
influence one like a strain of music."

Laid along the shore of an Adirondack lake, a corduroy track dominates Régis Gignoux' Log Road in Hamilton County, New York. Though the road blends harmoniously with the woody shore, the area was no longer virgin wilderness when it was painted in 1844.

Discovered in the 1960s in a cell͏ in Troy, New York, Charles Cromwe͏ Ingham's work entitled The Gre͏ Adirondack Pass—Painted on the Sp͏ was almost certainly a product of h͏ 1837 expedition to the Adirondack͏. Today the area is named Indian Pas͏

In Thomas Cole's *Schroon Mountain*, the peak looms majestically above *Schroon Lake. The mood of the picture suggests the powerful,*

almost fearful emotions experienced by these 19th Century artists in the Adirondack wilderness.

2/ The Inland Sea

Thus it came about that the valley with its long, narrow waters and the neighboring, difficult ranges, stamped its own distinct imprint on the history of a continent. F. VAN DE WATER/ LAKE CHAMPLAIN AND LAKE GEORGE

It is 6:15 a.m. on a morning in mid-February, and I am standing on the west shore of Lake Champlain, looking eastward to the long, dark spine of the Green Mountains of Vermont. The temperature is 10° below zero. Venus, the morning star, has risen and is climbing to the point where it will soon vanish in the glare of the ascending sun. The sky is just beginning to glow with a faint silvery sheen. Some of the reflected light glimmers on the frozen surface of the lake. The ice has hardened for several weeks since the first freeze and is now more than 10 inches thick, strong enough to support the Jeeps hauling out the ice-fishing shanties that produce an annual winter catch of Lake Champlain smelt —small, sweet vestiges of past eons when this great fresh-water body was an inland arm of the sea. Only a few days ago the ice was black and bare and people of the valley were aglide on skates upon a mirrored rink extending for miles north and south and from shore to shore. But then snow descended, and this morning the ice lies under a white counterpane 14 inches deep.

Now it is 6:45 and the sky begins to exercise its command of the spectrum: pale green ripens into peach, then lemon and finally robin's-egg blue. But dawn has not yet descended to earth. The mountains still present a black profile sequined by only a few points of light from lonely farmhouses at the foot of the range. Ten minutes later the still-sunken sun spotlights above the silhouette of the mountains a curious flotilla of clouds, each long and cylindrical, extended on a north-south axis and totally black, as black as the range beneath them, perhaps six or eight in all. Overhead the sky is crystalline. Some of the clouds look to me—as I stand shivering in the cold, transfixed by the beauty of the morning—like the pike and pickerel in the waters of Lake Champlain, mouths agape and fins flaring.

At 7:15 the sun explodes, a great fireball above the long ridge of the range. The black clouds change color and shape. They now float above the lake as lightly as the elm-bark canoes of the lake's original proprietors, the Iroquois, or the birch-bark canoes of their arch-enemies, the Algonquin and Huron of Canada. The sun soars higher and lays a crimson carpet across the snowy surface of the lake. And in the chill wind that always stirs with the rising of the sun, I remember as I watch the widening wound of sun on ice that this fair and most beautiful lake is the bloodiest lake in the history of our land, a true wilderness battleground.

At the beginning of the 17th Century the first of the lake's white war-makers, Samuel de Champlain, unfurled the fleur-de-lis at Quebec and claimed that province and all of Canada for the French crown; the following year, he made his personal discovery of the lake and named it for himself. From then until the end of the War of 1812, Lake Champlain —deep, wide, an inland waterway almost perfectly designed as an invasion route—witnessed a succession of bitter clashes. In the 17th Century conquering Frenchmen contended with Indians for their lands and the fur pelts that were to become the basis of a rich commercial empire for the Europeans. In the 18th Century Frenchman fought Briton —with Indians on both sides—to defend that empire, and lost. When the English colonies revolted against British power on the continent, raw American levies with improvised fleets battled regulars—and a 35-year-old general named Benedict Arnold, doubling as a naval commander, won a significant victory. Finally, in 1812, the British returned, their object to gain control of the upper reaches of the Saint Lawrence and a strategic stranglehold over the new nation.

Most beautiful, most bloody—what other lake in America can compare with Lake Champlain? Each of the more than 2,000 other lakes in the Adirondacks has its own passionate lovers. Lake George, whose stately mountains rise directly from rocky shores, so moved the Jesuit missionary, Père Isaac Jogues, that he named it for the Eucharist—Lac du Saint Sacrement. The British later named the lake for George II. Schroon Lake, a few miles to the west, has been compared to Italy's lovely mountain-ringed Lake Como. But my heart lies with Champlain; to my eyes the broad and spacious sweep of its valley appears to have been created by a master landscape artist. Champlain's perspectives and horizontal distances, the gracious expanse of water cradled between two distant mountain ranges 70 miles apart, provide vistas that are both noble and undemanding.

The longitudinal profile of Lake Champlain appears rather like that of a deformed carrot with a long, thin taproot at the south. Its feeder stream, Wood Creek, the narrow tail of the taproot, provided the warring Indians and early colonial armies with a few extra miles of waterway on the inland route between the Hudson and Saint Lawrence rivers. The lake's current flows indolently northward for a distance of 125 miles, through a profusion of islands at the upper end to an outlet via the Richelieu River into the Saint Lawrence northeast of Montreal.

Lake Champlain has other feeder streams coming in from both sides —from Vermont on the east and New York State on the west. Historically the most important tributary is the narrow Lake George outlet, which connects the two lakes at a place the Iroquois called Ticonderoga *(where the waters meet)* and gave Indians and colonial armies an alternative water route to and from the upper Hudson River a few miles south.

Here, by Champlain's own hand, first blood was drawn between Indians and whites in the region. A white man's fort, built in the 1750s on a headland above the narrows, changed hands during the French and Indian Wars, falling to a soldier of the British king, Lord Jeffrey Amherst. Later it was captured in the American Revolution by a mixed force of Ethan Allen's Green Mountain Boys and Continental troops.

Before the advent of Champlain and the stains of battle, the lake's shores had been glimpsed by another Frenchman, this one on a peaceful mission of exploration. He was Jacques Cartier, an adventurous Breton mariner who obtained a commission from his sovereign, Francis I, to discover a northwest passage to the Orient. Between 1534 and 1541 Cartier made three voyages to the New World. He found no diamonds, no gold, but he did discover, explore and name the lower reaches of the Saint Lawrence.

During his second voyage, having sailed up the river beyond the great rock of Quebec, Cartier arrived at an Indian village beneath another imposing promontory, and on the morning of October 3, 1535, was led by friendly guides to the summit of this high hill, which he named Mont

A March sun sinking behind the Adirondacks glistens on ice sheathing the waters of Lake Champlain—for 200 years a theater of war.

Royal. What he saw dismayed him, for below in the great curve of the river boiled the white fury of the impassable rapids now known as Lachine—an ironic name implying that above them lay the legendary passage to China. Cartier then looked southward and saw an unbroken sweep of primeval pine forest and in the remote distance an expanse of blue water that may have been Lake Champlain.

For more than half a century after Cartier's first glimpse of the Champlain Valley, its waters were traversed only by Indian hunting and war parties. Today, a blue and gold historical marker stands at Ticonderoga. There the southern taproot of the lake begins to widen, a place where no vessel could pass unobserved by day. The marker recalls the arrival of the first white men actually to reach the lake, and the consequences of that arrival: "Near here on July 30, 1609, Samuel de Champlain, aided by two Frenchmen and Huron and Montagnais allies, defeated a band of Iroquois warriors."

Champlain had traveled many miles for this small battle. Born in Brouage, a fishing port south of Brittany, he developed in his youth a love of the sea and a wanderlust. In his lifetime he made 29 crossings of the Atlantic—14 round trips and a final one-way journey before he died in Quebec on Christmas Day, 1635. It was during his sixth voyage that he had his fateful confrontation with the Iroquois at Ticonderoga.

In the light of what flowed from that encounter the message of the historical marker is, to say the least, laconic. And it is difficult today, as one stands on the gently sloping grassy bank amid maples, oaks, birches and other deciduous trees that have replaced the once-towering white pines, to envisage this pastoral setting as a spot where, in one fierce minute of combat, a century and more of implacable warfare among Indians and white men was launched. In a few seconds, these Indians first felt the impact of the destructive technology and the unrelenting ambition that were to destroy them as a people.

Our knowledge of the event comes from Champlain himself. On June 28, 1609, according to his own account, Champlain had started south into the domain of the Iroquois with a group of his own men and his Huron, Algonquin and Montagnais allies, aware that only by sharing the Canadian Indians' warfare could he win their loyalty. "The country becomes more and more beautiful as you advance," he wrote, "covered with great and high forest." Entering the lake, Champlain and his party paddled by day and camped by night. As they progressed farther south, deeper into the domain of the enemy, they reversed the rhythm of their schedule, proceeding under cover of darkness, hiding in the deep evergreen woods by day. They were advancing toward the narrows at Ticonderoga after nightfall. And there on July 29 they encountered the enemy, a war party of the Iroquois, encamped for the night on the meadow beneath the bluff on which Fort Ticonderoga now stands.

All night long the warriors exchanged noisy insults, boasts and threats. At daybreak Champlain and his two companions landed without opposition, screened from the enemy by their escort of friendly warriors. Two of the Frenchmen slipped into the woods. Champlain remained in the rear of the main force. Then, according to his narrative, some 200 Iroquois emerged from their camp—"strong, robust men, who came slowly to meet us with a gravity and calm which I admired, and at their head were three chiefs," distinguished by the eagle feathers in their hair. Champlain himself wore light armor and a helmet topped by a white plume.

As the Iroquois advanced, the Canadian Indians opened their ranks so that Champlain might stand revealed to them. They froze in mute amazement. "I looked at them," Champlain wrote, "and they looked at me. When I saw them getting ready to shoot their arrows at us, I leveled my arquebus (a handgun fired by a match), which I had loaded with four balls, and aimed straight at one of the three chiefs. The shot brought down two and wounded another. On this, our Indians set up such a yelling that one could not have heard a thunder-clap, and . . . arrows flew thick on both sides. The Iroquois were greatly astonished and frightened to see two of their men killed so quickly (and), seeing their chief dead, they abandoned the field and fled into the depth of the forest. Our Indians also killed several and took ten or twelve prisoners." The battle was over.

For three hours after the rout of the Iroquois, the Canadian Indians celebrated their triumph—singing, dancing and feasting on the abandoned supplies of their foes. During this interval, Champlain reconnoitered the sickle-shaped inlet of Ticonderoga Creek, hopeful that his party could continue southward to the river that led down to the sea. But on his return he found that the flush of victory had faded fast; his Indian allies feared the Iroquois too greatly to venture farther into their territory and the haste of their departure was akin to flight. For the next 24 hours the flotilla paddled northward nonstop. When they finally came ashore Champlain witnessed for the first time, with horror that must have rivaled that of the Iroquois on see-

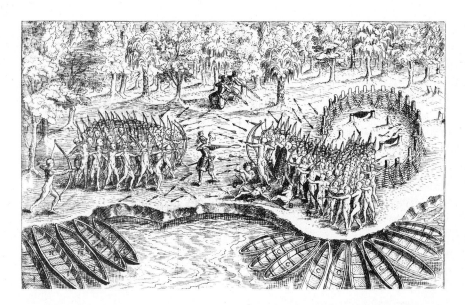

Samuel Champlain's engraved illustration shows him clad in full armor and plumed helmet at the head of his Algonquin, Montagnais and Huron allies, firing the shot from his arquebus that was to bring down three Iroquois chiefs and earn for the French the enmity of that nation. Following the conventions of the day, the Indians are shown naked though they were actually clothed, and the engraver has airily changed their canoes into French river boats, while a few palm trees enliven the background.

ing the lethal close-range effects of firearms, the aftermath of Indian battle. He reported the event as follows:

"Having gone about eight leagues, the Indians, towards evening, took one of the prisoners . . . and burned this poor wretch a little at a time in order to make him suffer the greater torment. . . . They begged me repeatedly to take fire and do like them. . . . When they saw that I was not pleased, they . . . told me to give him a shot with the arquebus. I did so, without his perceiving anything, and with one shot caused him to escape all the tortures he would have suffered."

There was both reward and retribution in the aftermath of the battle. The reward lay in the lasting loyalty of the Canadian Indians, who aided the French in opening to Champlain and his successors the western route to the Great Lakes and a monopoly of the fur trade. Retribution lay in the hostility of the Iroquois toward the French: the Iroquois were to become allies of the British, who would win Canada a century and a half later.

Following Champlain's adventure at Ticonderoga, the great inland sea again receded from the white man's line of history, navigated only by the war canoes of the Iroquois bound northward to ravage their Canadian kin and attack their new foes, the French. Yet despite the Iroquois' fury a few Jesuit missionaries persisted in attempting to convert them to Christianity. The first of these missionaries was

Isaac Jogues, a shy and gentle native of Orléans who had come to New France in 1636 to work among the Huron on Georgian Bay. On August 2, 1642, returning to his mission after a supply trip to Quebec with two young lay assistants and 22 converted Huron, he was ambushed by a flotilla of Iroquois raiders near Trois Rivières on the Saint Lawrence. In the fight that followed, Père Jogues, being extraordinarily fleet of foot despite his apparent frailty, managed to escape and hide among reeds beside the river. Thence he watched the Iroquois make prisoners of his two countrymen and his Indian converts. Well aware of what lay in store for them—and what would be his own fate—he emerged from his hiding place and surrendered. And then began a long trail to the south, following the same route Champlain had traversed 33 years earlier, up the Saint Lawrence, up the Richelieu River and into the tranquil valley of Lake Champlain.

On the eighth day, Jogues' captors met another Iroquois war party heading north and they joined forces for an evening of celebration. Of this encounter, Jogues later wrote, "We were obliged to sustain a new shock. It is a belief among those barbarians that those who go to war are the more fortunate in proportion as they are cruel toward their enemies." The scene of the celebration and of Jogues' first truly dreadful night of torture may have been a small wooded island in a cove on the western shore of Lake Champlain about three miles south of Westport Bay. This islet, roughly the size of a jagged and irregular football field, has been known as Jogues' Island as long as most natives of the Champlain Valley can remember. I cannot count the number of times when as a boy I swam around it, canoed around it, camped upon it. And on one bright afternoon this last winter a friend of mine and I walked out across the ice to look again on the little island's unspoiled beauty, to try to envisage what Père Jogues endured.

The shore of Jogues' Island is rocky and abrupt. We had to scramble to climb the steep and slippery bank, carpeted with pine needles frosted with snow, and attain the flat, mesa-like top of the island. Once there, among ancient white and red pines, hemlocks, spruces and balsam firs, and a few bare columns of red oaks, I found it impossible to conceive of this island gem as a theater of torture.

It had been August when Père Jogues was taken there and forced to run the gantlet, naked, between two lines of warriors armed with sharp and thorny branches. "There was a rivalry among them," he wrote, "to discharge upon us the most and the heaviest blows; they made me march last, that I might be more exposed to their rage. I had not accomplished the half of this course when I fell to the earth under the weight of that hail and of those redoubled blows. When I was restored to my senses, they began their assault over again . . . and when strength failed me, they applied fire to my arm and thighs."

Now, more than three centuries later, as my friend and I stood silently among the ancient trees of Jogues' Island, the late-winter sun began to burn out like a fading Indian campfire behind the foothills to the west. And so, clutching juniper and cedar branches, we executed a grand glissade down the snowy embankment to the lake below. As we walked across the ice toward the mainland, I thought back to the climax and denouement of Père Jogues' harrowing test of soul.

Continuing for two more days on their way up the lake, captors and captives reached a portage where, despite his festering wounds, Jogues was forced to carry heavy loads of the Iroquois' booty. At one point the healthy Indians, hurrying onward, put such a distance between themselves and Jogues that he realized he had an opportunity to escape. But his converts were ahead and he decided, "I would rather have suffered all sorts of torments than abandon to death those whom I could somewhat console and upon whom I could confer the blood of my Savior through the Sacraments of His Church." So he staggered on.

After a year of captivity, during which the Iroquois treated him as a slave, the Dutch at Fort Orange—Albany—learned of Jogues' plight and compassionately ransomed him for 600 guilders' worth of goods. Jogues spent three years in France recovering from his ordeal. Yet his missionary fervor would not let him rest. In 1646 he returned to Quebec and, determined to convert his torturers to the Christian faith, made his way southward again into Iroquois territory, announcing as he bade farewell, "I go back to die."

On this, his final journey, Père Jogues met no hostility en route and was even received with courtesy at the Iroquois village where he had been held captive. But the omens were bad that year. There had been drought; crops had failed; the Indians were suspicious of the mysteries of Jogues' religion. On October 18, 1646, as Jogues bent forward to enter his tent, an Iroquois warrior shattered his skull with a tomahawk.

A few weeks after my expedition across the ice to Jogues' Island, I went to explore another historic island, about 40 miles to the north, that, for all its patina of past events, remains, like Jogues' Island, relatively untouched by 20th Century man. Such is Valcour Island, where the Revolutionary War Battle of Valcour Bay was fought on October

11, 1776. (It was probably near here, too, that Champlain dispatched the tortured Iroquois with his arquebus.) Almost two miles long and more than half a mile wide, Valcour is much larger than Jogues' Island; indented and scalloped with many coves and small bays, Valcour is elevated at the southern end with limestone cliffs.

This time, while we were crossing the frozen surface (my companions were Dr. Philip C. Walker, Professor of Biology at the State University of New York at Plattsburgh and the leading expert on the island, and Wayne H. Byrne, Chairman of the Adirondack Conservancy Committee), we tried to envision that morning in the autumn following the Declaration of Independence, when Benedict Arnold lay in wait with his small American flotilla for a larger British fleet en route south from Canada to invade the fledgling republic. From information supplied by scouts Arnold knew that he was outnumbered—some 700 British sailors and soldiers against perhaps 500 Americans. But Arnold cleverly had chosen to position his vessels between Valcour Island and the mainland shore where the channel is so narrow that the British fleet would have difficulty in bringing more than a few of their ships at a time to battle.

As we walked across the channel there was meltwater under our feet and the ice groaned ominously as we advanced, for there had been a February thaw. Halfway to the island we came upon some fishermen who had cut holes in the ice and were bringing forth a generous haul of smelt. We asked them about the thickness of the ice and they said three inches—safe enough to walk upon. So we continued on our way across the channel, talking of that moment when Arnold's gunboats, stationed exactly where we now stood, espied the oncoming British squadron, under the command of General Sir Guy Carleton.

Screened as the Americans were by a small headland north of their position, the British failed to sight them. Running before a strong northerly breeze, Carleton's force sailed blithely past the island off its outer shore—unaware, until too late, of the American ambush. This ineptitude cost the British their advantageous windward position, and they had to put about and claw back up around the southern tip of the island and into the teeth of the north wind to engage the American fleet, drawn up in a shallow crescent facing south. Once joined, the battle raged for five hours. When darkness fell, no American gunboat or barge had escaped damage; 60 men were killed or injured. Carleton reported his casualties at eight killed and six wounded—in the opinion of most historians today an understatement. Despite the odds against him, Arnold's tactics had paid off; he had not beaten the British, but he had avoided disaster. The enemy drew off and, under cover of darkness, blessed by the continuing north wind, Arnold slipped his fleet southward. But the wind was fluky; Sir Guy and his flotilla caught Arnold before he reached Crown Point. Arnold burned his boats rather than surrender them to the British, and made his way overland to Ticonderoga. This stronghold might well have been taken by the British. But Carleton had no taste for a winter campaign, and made his way back to Quebec. The threat of invasion was over.

When my two conservationist friends and I had crossed the frozen channel, we emerged on meadowland that had been cleared many years ago and was reverting to brush and forest growth. The latitude of Valcour Island lies within the range of the eastern deciduous forest zone, generally dominated by beech, birch and maple, interspersed with conifers. At its northeastern end the woods are mixed heavily with hemlock, white pine, spruce, balsam fir and white cedar.

As we walked amid the diversified growth, through brushy areas studded with saplings, through conifers and hardwoods along the central axis of the island, and finally through the pure stands of conifers along the eastern and southern shores, I asked Dr. Walker why in addition to the battle he had found Valcour Island so fascinating.

"What makes Valcour Island a rarity within the Adirondack Park," he replied, "is that some of its flora is like that of the high peaks at an altitude of 2,500 to 3,500 feet. The elevation of Lake Champlain above sea level is barely 95 feet. Perhaps you can add another 90 feet for the cliffs at the south end of the island, and a few higher elevations in the central parts."

"Well then," I asked, "given a near-sea-level elevation, how do you account for the alpine-like vegetation?"

"The winds. Valcour Island stands in a kind of wind tunnel. It's a small island and has no protection from the winter winds. Even in summer the winds are cold. Sometimes the escarpment at the south end is battered by waves four to five feet high. The vegetation shows a reaction to this. It's a harsh climatic condition. Furthermore, the water around the island, which lies in the broadest part of Lake Champlain and is quite deep, takes a long time to warm up in spring."

Walker pointed to the pines on the east shore of the island and noted that, though tall, they did not stand erect. "They become covered with ice in winter," he explained, "and tilt in a lopsided fashion from the

The eastern side of Valcour Island (left) and Spoon Island appear as they would have to a lookout in the stern of a ship in the British fleet that sailed south on Lake Champlain in 1776. The British, looking for an American flotilla under Benedict Arnold, failed to spot the enemy ships drawn up in a channel to the west of the island, and had to turn and tack against the wind in order to engage the Americans.

combined action of wind and ice. On the other hand, the firs stand straight because of the quality of their wood." We wandered now to the brink of the escarpment and gazed down its sheer wall to the frozen lake below. "See that white cedar, the arbor vitae at the base of this cliff?" Walker went on. "That's the first line of defense. It clings to the cliff for dear life with deep-running, wide-spreading roots and it screens the other conifers, the birches and the maples and the beeches above it, from the wind."

As we stood now, looking south from the top of the escarpment, Walker added that another factor in Valcour's unusual vegetation was the brevity of the growing season. "Up here," he said, "we have only 144 frost-free days a year. By up here I mean north of Lake George. Between Saratoga and Lake George something like 40 species of woody plants disappear—it's too cold for them. That's why in the Adirondacks we have few sycamores, no sweet or sour gum, and only a little flowering dogwood."

By now we had climbed to the highest point of land on Valcour Island and found ourselves atop a cliff almost 100 feet high, a fascinating construction of sedimentary limestone, tilted like the other formations on the island slightly toward the east. It was here, as we stood in a leafless grove of birches and maples on the edge of the escarpment, looking southward down the lake, that my other companion, Wayne Byrne, called my attention to clusters of very large birds' nests—some as much as six feet across—with which the bare branches were festooned.

"What you see here," he said, "is one of the major blue heron rookeries in the northeast. It has been here, we think, for about 200 years; because of the island's isolation, the nests remain undisturbed from year to year. Right now the herons have migrated south." I wished that they were currently in residence; the blue heron is a magnificent bird with a broad wingspread equal to that of the average bald eagle—more than six feet in many cases.

In addition to the blue heron, Valcour Island also provides sanctuary for ducks of all sorts throughout the open-water months, as well as for many mammals—white-tailed deer, snowshoe hares, cottontail rabbits, squirrels, weasels, foxes, field mice. In fact, added Byrne, "just about everything you'll find in this latitude and climate, though there aren't very many of each type. But in a region like the Adirondacks, which doesn't have much wildlife to begin with, the island is a protected spot for all these species."

The sun was sinking over the mountains, so we began our trek back across the ice to the mainland shore. The fishermen had enjoyed a beneficent day. Their buckets glittered with shiny smelt, slithering and flipping in efforts to escape.

Retracing my steps across the ice from the island, the place seemed to me, in its present isolation and its embattled past, a summation of Lake Champlain. Beautiful in its fragments of turquoise, of emerald, of lapis lazuli—capes, headlands, islands, coves—the shores of the entire lake had once been as Valcour still remains. Like that one small island, all had been remote—every part of the valley a sanctuary for heron or fox as determined by such matters as food supply or safety from predators. When the white men had come, they had fought over the lake, but only because it was there—a way of getting quickly from one part of the continent to another. Long though it lasted, the fighting did finally stop—after the Battle of Plattsburgh, when on September 11, 1814, American forces beat the British in a decisive contest that ended the War of 1812.

Even today there still remains a way to envision the whole valley of Lake Champlain as it was when it was still all wilderness—and still a battleground. On the east side of Lake Champlain stands a long, low, flat-ridged mountain a bit northwest of Middlebury, Vermont. An abandoned lumber road winds its way up this small promontory, and from a bare, rocky outlook on the summit one can see the lake's great expanse, from its taproot in the south, through the strategic, embattled narrows at Ticonderoga and Crown Point, to the island clusters off Plattsburgh and beyond and to the distant cube of Mount Royal.

But even more dramatic is the panorama as you look directly west, especially in the evening as the sun declines behind the high, forbidding dome of the Adirondack massif. From this point you see directly below your feet the friendly checkerboard fields and farms of the Vermont dairylands. Then farther west you espy the blue sweep of Lake Champlain. And beyond that, the great buttress of the Adirondack uplift, where even the Iroquois seldom ventured, and that until the turn of the 19th Century was known as the Dismal Wilderness. Only the very brave ventured westward, seeking a pass among these high peaks to perhaps gentler lands in the haze of the setting sun.

NATURE WALK / On Haystack Mountain

PHOTOGRAPHS BY ROBERT WALCH

We reached the foot of the Lower Ausable Lake a few minutes before 9 o'clock on the perfect morning we had waited for. A cold front had blown through in the night and dispersed the autumn haze that had overhung the mountains for a week. In its train the front had left frost and a sprinkling of snow that now, like a bridal veil, powdered the red-gold mantle of the October woods.

There is no more dramatic scene in the Adirondacks, whatever the hour or season, than the one that bursts upon the hiker encountering his first glimpse of the lake. The road to its shoreline winds uphill through a three-mile forested corridor and then, rounding a blind curve, drops steeply to a small beach. The moment is like the lifting of a curtain, disclosing a long, narrow, glacial lake, with cliffs rising vertically on either side. They are wooded at the base; naked rock lies above. No foot trail traverses the shore; as in a fjord the only passage is by boat.

On this glittery morning the Lower Lake was our water gate to Mount Haystack, our objective for the day. Though only third in altitude among the Adirondack mountains, Haystack is well worth climbing. It ranks first, with those who have scaled it,

for the unsurpassed view discernible from its peak.

There are summit routes other than the one we planned to take from the Lower Ausable, but they are longer and less interesting. Besides, I have always liked the idea of starting and ending this challenging climb by water. I have always liked it, too, in October, for that is the best mountain month. The fall colors are riotous. The forest canopy has partially opened to clear the views. And, despite the prospect of returning in darkness—the hours of October daylight fade swiftly, and dusk in the forest is night—to me, the beauty of the Adirondacks on such a day as this would be more than ample reward for the autumnal hazards of the ascent to the peak.

By the time we reached the boathouse at the southern end of the lake, the rising sun had already crested the cliffs on the lake's southeast side, and lighted the white-dusted birches and conifers clinging to the opposite shoreline. Hurriedly, somewhat later than planned, we drew our Adirondack guide boat, a sturdy kind of canoe equipped with oars, into the water and began the two-mile pull that would take us to the upper end of the lake.

The morning air hung blissfully still. Not a golden leaf or green spruce bough stirred on the steep slopes above us. The lake's surface was a black mirror reflecting the paper birches and sugar maples crowding the shore. And we had indeed found the perfect day. For it is well known to experienced Adirondack

A CANADA GOOSE

travelers that the long rocky ravine that contains the lake can be a wind tunnel, with the wind always ahead —against you going out in the morning, then reversing itself and opposing you again on your late-afternoon return. But today we were in luck. Not a breeze riffled the surface.

We glided along the shore in silence broken only by the dipping of the oars. No birds sang, no trout leaped. And then, as we rounded a rocky point of land, we saw a lone Canada goose, separated somehow from its migrating flock, floating indifferently in a shallow cove. It

SUGAR MAPLES AND PAPER BIRCHES ON THE LOWER AUSABLE LAKE

cocked a cautious eye at our intrusive boat but disdained flight. We were lucky to spot the goose—ordinarily, the lake is virtually lifeless —cold and deep and devoid of aquatic vegetation. Even in midsummer the water is somber, dark with minerals brought to the lake by the brooks and falls that feed it from the slopes of the mountains above.

High above our heads, perpendicular rock faces caught the slanting rays of the sun and deflected them into dikes and crevices, creating gargoyles that glowered at their shadows on the rock piles below. Only the straight white candles of the birch trees, tipped with the flaming wicks of their expiring leaves, lent interior light to the scene.

Hiking The Carry

It took nearly an hour to row the length of the lake—a comparatively slow passage of the Lower Ausable, but not bad since I was rowing and especially because the final quarter mile involves some tricky navigation through big boulders and underwater snags. Landing at 9:40 a.m., we pulled our boat ashore, shouldered our packs and set off along what is known as The Carry—a level mile of lovely trail that flanks the rapids between the Upper and Lower Ausable Lakes. The sun struck diamonds from the water and topaz from the beech, red spruce and maple above. The lightly frozen ground crunched beneath our feet and, beside the path, ice crystals glinted on seedlings and blades of grass.

We crossed several log bridges over tributary streams and walked

RED SPRUCE AND A BEECH AT THE LAKE'S NARROWS

alternately on through woods and grassy glades. I remembered that in these small meadows I had several times seen deer. Later in the season they would gather here for shelter against the winter cold, but no white tail twitched today. On one fallen yellow birch log we saw puffballs, an aptly named fungus. When struck —by a blown branch or a passing creature—they discharge spores in a smoky cloud. Considering our time-table, we did not linger to watch them perform today.

The trail was carpeted with leaves and, from time to time, we stopped to inspect them—scarlet, magenta and gold strewn on the ground in fragments that created a mosaic. At around 10 a.m. we arrived at the base of the mountain, where we were still some distance from the hard part of the morning's ascent.

PUFFBALLS ON A FALLEN BIRCH

Haystack is a seducer. The climb starts gently with what the Adirondack Mountain Club guidebook describes as a moderate grade. The novice does not know that after two hours of steady and not too demanding ascent through woods and across small purling brooks, the mountain assumes the character of a fortification, defying the climber to scale its upper reaches. But we had met the

RED-MAPLE LEAVES ON A DECAYING LOG

challenge of Haystack many times before, and were aware that we would have to maintain a brisk pace to cover the ascent of 3,070 feet in a horizontal distance of 4.35 miles. And we could waste no time coming down; otherwise we would be in trouble. The temperature that morning was in the 20s—it would undoubtedly be 20° or lower in the evening, and we had brought along no gear for an overnight stay. But now the sun was high and warm, and as we started to climb we peeled off some of the outer clothes we had needed earlier in the day.

During the first hour we walked easily through a beautiful stand of hardwood, columned with maples and shaggy yellow birch. The forest canopy shed a golden light upon us for the first mile and a half of our ascent. Off to our right we could hear the water of Shanty Brook chattering as it raced down from its hidden sources high above on the mountainside. A lone beech, its blue-gray bark mottled with darker bands, thrust upward on one side of the trail, silhouetted against the sunlight filtered down through yellow leaves. Where its roots fed into the ground cover, mosses spread themselves, their emerald green in vivid contrast with the deep russet of the beech leaves scattered around the tree's base.

Farther ahead lay a wind-felled branch, where a hickory tussock moth caterpillar sunned itself in the final stage of its larval life. It was the first living creature we had spotted since we had left the Canada goose on the Lower Ausable. As the

A SOLITARY BEECH TRUNK BY THE TRAIL

days shortened, it would begin spinning the winter cocoon in which it would lie dormant over the cold months, to emerge in June metamorphosed into a night-roaming moth with wings that span nearly two and one half inches.

At around 3,000 feet, we entered a zone where balsam, red spruce and hemlock began to intermingle with the deciduous trees, and the whole character of the woodland changed. Yellow foliage began to yield to dark green, and the trail, no longer dappled with fallen leaves, lay dark and moist, embroidered at its edges by a tapestry of ferns.

A Panoply of Mosses

Here and there the spraddled roots of a balsam clutched a moss-covered boulder. In fact, mosses and fungi were everywhere—on the trunks of great trees, on fallen timber blown down by the hurricane of 1950, on every rocky outcrop. The bright emerald of sphagnum caught my eye, as did the silvery green of cushion moss, the dainty feathers of knight's

A TUSSOCK MOTH CATERPILLAR

plume and the translucent leaves of eurhynchium, growing on the underwater masonry of the streams we occasionally crossed. I was especially taken with the perky club mosses. Like tiny Christmas trees only two inches high, they poked their spires upward amid clusters of pale green ferns and seedling firs.

For the next half hour we traveled on the level, moving over a spongy duff trail in the half-light of midday, winding our way around boulders covered with green lichens, treading on the unsteady stones that lay in the beds of innumerable brooks. The forest darkened as the evergreens closed their needled curtains overhead. And now, about halfway to the summit, we found the snowfall of the preceding night lying all around us, bleaching the balsam boughs and spruce. Icicles dangled from every ledge; in our ascent we had advanced the calendar a full season, from fall to winter.

The grade remained kindly until a spot where, through a rent in the forest canopy, we caught a glimpse of Little Haystack, a subsidiary rock cone that protrudes from the north shoulder of its parent peak. Through another opening we could look off to the east and the southeast and obtain a glimpse of the profiles of the neighboring mountain peaks—Sawtooth, Nippletop, Colvin and Blake.

MOSSES ADORNING THE BASE OF A BEECH

LENZITES FUNGI ON A BEECH LOG

A GROVE OF RED SPRUCE AND BALSAM FIR

And around noon we came upon the noisy rapids of Haystack Brook that, for the last half mile, we had heard but not seen, and lingered momentarily beside its bank to catch our breath and drink its ice-cold water.

After that, the climb became more arduous. The path veered sharply left and headed straight up toward the main range trail that takes off from the summit of Marcy, plunges directly across Panther Gorge and thence traverses the tops of all the central peaks—Haystack, Basin, Saddleback, Gothics, Armstrong and Wolf Jaws—before arriving at last in the haven of Keene Valley. The pitch was so steep that we had to pause frequently to catch our breath. Attacking the slope, we perspired despite the snow and ice around us. It astonished me to see trees clinging to a hill so precipitous. But the conifers marched upward with us.

Four times we reached sheer rock ledges, unscalable without expert mountaineering equipment—or ladders. At each site the Adirondack Trail Improvement Society had provided ladders built of stout cedar logs. These helped us surmount the obstacles without recourse to pitons, ropes and axes. We met the junction of the main range trail at 1:30 p.m. and relaxed briefly for lunch in a sheltering lean-to.

At this height the temperature was still in the 20s. Although we could see our breath, the sun was golden and in its glow we forgot the chill. Beds of slender anomodon and common haircap moss lay nearby, lightly dusted with snow and, not far away,

ANOMODON MOSSES ON ICY ROCKS

A SPRIG OF BALSAM FIR

BUNCHBERRY ON SPHAGNUM MOSS

MELTING SNOW CRYSTALS ON HAIRCAP MOSS

bunchberry grew out of a carpeting of sphagnum moss.

At about 2 p.m. we resumed the last leg of the climb. This was by any measure the most exhausting part of the trip. The lunch break had relaxed our muscles. We knew the summit was close, though invisible from our vantage point, but now for a half hour the trail offered an agonizing ascent over an old, eroded stream bed, filled with loose rocks, slippery with moss and ice.

Up to Timberline

Each step was difficult, and we picked our way carefully. The familiar hazard to all climbers, a sprained ankle, loomed in the perspective of the scant five hours of daylight that remained. We pushed on through a stunted growth of red spruce and balsam, balancing ourselves at times with the help of branches beside the trail. Some of the trees to which we clung, though a century old, were only three feet high, stunted by the winds of winter. They were virgin trees, ignored because of their size and remoteness by the lumbermen who devastated the Adirondacks in the 19th Century.

As always, when nearing the summit of a mountain, I began to hurry, anticipating the moment when we would emerge from the scrub forest onto open rock. At 2:30 in the afternoon, as the spruce and balsam beside the trail thinned out and diminished in size, and the ever-opening sky lured us upward, we crossed the timberline. The last of the dwarf conifers now lay behind us and we found ourselves at the

MOSSES AND LICHENS ON WEATHERED ROCKS

base of Little Haystack, a formidable pyramid of rock that we had to scale before attacking the final height. Its ramparts were almost perpendicular, devoid of vegetation except for a mixture of lichens and mosses. But in the rock face were fissures and handholds that helped us follow a route marked with cairns to Little Haystack's top.

From this narrow pedestal we caught our first view of the range. Although we were tempted to linger, the hour was late. The sun was dropping. A few high cirrus clouds appeared, and a cold breath of air crept under our shirts, warning us that evening was on its way. Nervous as any Adirondack man can be at the imminent loss of light at this season of the year, I said we must move on quickly. My friend said the light was more beautiful minute by

minute, the colors were concentrating. Could we stay on for perhaps another 20 minutes, 10 minutes? Total darkness, I knew, would descend no later than 7 p.m. Reluctantly, we resumed our trek.

Ahead of us loomed the climactic mass of Big Haystack; to conquer it we had first to descend the southern face of Little Haystack into a col filled with spruces.

To the Summit

Stone cairns guided us down a precipice that sometimes allowed no more than two or three inches for foot- and handholds. Shortly we found ourselves in the col confronting the ultimate peak. Before us we saw a less perpendicular approach glazed with the ice and snow of the night before, icicles dangling from ledges of weathered rock and glimmering in the lowering sun.

The last assault took less time than we had anticipated. We scrambled up over a succession of ledges upholstered with a springy jungle consisting of alpine plants with tangled branches and miniature leaves that exist only on the loftiest mountaintops of the High Peaks—Lapland rosebay, bearberry willow and a number of grasses.

But we soon raised our eyes from the matted shrubs beneath us, for now we were close to the goal. Despite our excitement and the descent of the sun in the western sky, we paused a moment to breathe, to glance eastward along the unfolding crenelations of the main range, and

FISSURES NEAR THE PEAK

to anticipate the total panorama we would shortly see after scaling the final height that still blocked the vistas to the south.

Each of the High Peaks offers its individual glories. From the summit of Marcy, for example, the Adiron-

THE BASE OF LITTLE HAYSTACK

dacks fade into infinity like a great sea of blue, undulating swells. But the view from Haystack, by contrast, reveals the mountains in dramatic intimacy. Though we were still below the summit, our eyes were already taking in two unforgettable sights: to the west, the mural of Marcy above Panther Gorge; to the east, the stark geometry of Gothics, a mountain whose summit is virtually bare of forest cover.

At 3:15 p.m., we reached Haystack's summit rock. In its crevices grew sedges and rushes, most notably a straw-colored rush called deer's hair. Around us we saw the final quadrant of the encompassing mountains. Here on the pinnacle of Haystack we were standing in the very heart of the Adirondack wilderness, seeing 27 of the major peaks marching across the horizon, their profiles chiseled by gorges and ravines, slide-scarred, blotched with the blue of lakes, bogs and ponds. Below us to the south lay the Ausable Lakes whence we had come, the long scalloped ridges of Colvin, Blake and Pinnacle above them, and part of the Dix massif in the distance far off to the left.

Though we had tasted our triumph but a moment, it was time to break the spell and start down the mountain—at once. Hurrying down Haystack's steep and treacherous south face, we found our boat and made our way through the shoals and out onto the lake to start the silent paddle homeward. Across the sky, the silhouette of a flight of geese, in V-formation, necks outthrust, arrowed toward the south. I hoped the lone goose we had seen earlier on the lake had rejoined its squadron.

DEER'S HAIR IN A SUMMIT CREVICE

LOOKING SOUTH FROM THE SUMMIT OF HAYSTACK

3/ The High Peaks

There is nothing constant in the universe,
All ebb and flow, and every shape that's born,
Bears in its womb the seeds of change.

OVID/ *METAMORPHOSES*

The drama started in midafternoon, June 29, 1963, when cumulus clouds began to weave together in white clumps over the corridor of Keene Valley some 20 miles west of Lake Champlain, and over Giant Mountain, eastern bulwark of the main range. Driven aloft by thermal updrafts, the clouds coalesced and thickened, billowing in towers of cumulonimbus six miles high. As the afternoon progressed, the cloud masses darkened and electrical forces came into play. The tension between clouds and earth became intolerable, then broke; lightning flashed and thunder echoed across the slopes and through mountain passes. At 4:45 p.m. the clouds burst asunder, sending down a six-inch torrent of rain —without recorded precedent in the Adirondacks.

The violence of the deluge was caused by a unique and fleeting condition of stagnation in the local weather pattern. In a normal thunderstorm, the epicenter moves, rotating counterclockwise and traveling slowly across country. In this case, the system stayed put, fed from all sides by hot, moisture-saturated, unstable air rushing up the steep ramparts of the mountain. The southwest wall of Giant is a funnel-shaped glacial cirque (a steep mountain amphitheater carved by ice) that may have been responsible for creating the shape of the entrapping air currents. In any event, for 90 minutes the clouds held a position about one mile square, directly over the summit of Giant, and in those 90 minutes disgorged their half a foot of rain water.

The effect of the storm was as startling as the rainfall itself. Below the summit the rain water drilled into the thin soil mantle. Each drop uncovered and exposed, little by little, the delicate roots of high-country plants and the precarious anchorage of dwarf spruce and balsam fir. Then, as the carpet of topsoil and vegetation became sodden, gravitation pried the mass of mud loose and shoved it ruthlessly down the mountainside. In the wake of such a mudslide everything goes—soil cover, plants, small trees, big trees—and as momentum builds, boulders join the jumbled avalanche, uprooting more trees, rending the forest canopy, blasting, bombarding, abrading the green mantle spun by slow centuries of growth.

And that is what happened on this black summer afternoon. The dreadful cataract of rock and mud and water and trees tobogganed downhill, spreading out through the woods of the lower slopes, gathering strength from its increase of overburden. As the velocity of the mudslide doubled, the transporting power of its tons of rock increased by a factor of 10 or 20, varying with the grade. Overwhelmed trees shed their bark and the wet soil ripped open, exposing decayed organic material and releasing a strong, sour stench.

Toward the base of Giant, where the slope began to level off, the great avalanche slowed. Yet its thrust was still powerful enough to sweep down to the valley floor, some 3,400 feet below the point where the slide began, depositing a barrier 10 to 15 feet deep across New York State Highway 73. In these violent moments the slow vegetative growth of centuries had been stripped away, leaving an enormous wound a few feet wide near the summit and spreading to 200 feet in width at the bottom of the mountain. Decades must pass before the processes of restoration work slowly outward across the blemish and mask it with a new tegument of green. On this day as the rain abated and the last few cobbles and pebbles came to rest, it was stunningly obvious that no mountain, indeed no range of mountains, can endure forever—that the "everlasting hills" of the Bible do not exist. There are no everlasting hills—not in the Adirondacks, not anywhere.

Erosion seldom takes such a dramatic form as Giant's mudslide, but it is always present, an unwearying, inexorable destroyer, whose main energizing force is gravity. No matter how durable or stable the façade of any mountainside may appear, or how thick its canopy of plants and trees may be, the entire soil mantle nevertheless creeps toward the valley floor like a dense, viscous liquid, bearing its plant cover with it.

For more than a billion years the degrading forces of nature have worked on the Adirondacks. These mountains survive today as the stumps of an ancient, far loftier and more imposing range, perhaps as high as the young Himalayas of today. They are the products of a billion years of alternating mountain building and erosion, uplift and leveling, rising and falling, creation and destruction by the hammering of rain, the wedges of frost and the scouring of mile-high sheets of ice.

But, for an eye blink, the slide on Giant made us aware of the usually unperceived processes of alteration in the profile of the land. To obtain a closer and more intimate view of the catastrophe I decided one day to follow the track of the great slide up the mountain to its headwall. So on a late-autumn weekend under gray skies that threatened snow, I joined a group of friends on a scramble up the avalanche path. That day, hovering clouds shrouded the crest of Giant. But we were not concerned with summit views; our interest lay in what was at our feet, and from the moment we left the highway we found ourselves in a wild, tilted corridor of mingled boulders and trees, shredded and shattered along the flank of the mountain.

It was not an easy climb, for the boulders and chunks of rock torn from the crags above were intermingled with small stones and pebbles that rolled and shifted under our feet. And at intervals beech and hemlock trees with bent or broken branches blocked the entire breadth of the slide. After two hours of ascent the grade steepened, the corridor narrowed, and we arrived finally at the base of the nearly vertical 1,000-foot cliff down which the avalanche had cut its first incision.

One young member of our party, an experienced mountaineer, was all for continuing up the precipice. But we had brought along no rock-climbing equipment, and at this moment big snowflakes began to feather lightly down. Broken, gashed, almost totally bare of greenery, the cliff looked to me like nothing so much as the scene of some frightful accident. And so it had been—a very brief and accidental chapter in the geological history of the place.

As we made our way off the mountain, I inspected the rocks more closely, and I recognized far older and even more powerful shaping forces. There were boulders eight feet or more in diameter deposited by the last great glacial advance. Others were jagged excisions from the cliffs and crags above us, torn out by the slide. But all had one quality in common—all seemed bland, homogenized, with drab colors, few sparkles and, significantly, no strata, no fossils. Why? Because the rocks were of igneous origin, intruded in a molten state into an existing layer of sed-

Resembling a broad, steep ski run on the side of Giant Mountain, a scar caused by a catastrophic mudslide glistens under fresh snow. The slide resulted from a record cloudburst that broke over the mountain in 1963.

imentary rock about a billion years ago. Here and there in the sedimentary rock small carbon or graphite flecks suggested that some very primitive soft marine plants or animals might once have inhabited the realm invaded by the igneous rock.

To a student of the rocks the stony corridor we traversed revealed a fascinating complexity of geology. For each and every one of these gray fragments of the planetary crust had endured more than a billion years of agonized ascent from the hot mantle of the earth, melting and crystallization, faulting and folding, uplift and erosion, resubmergence —and then reemergence on the surface, followed by renewed and constant battering from rain and frost, with episodic scouring and planing during the recurrent invasions of the ice sheets from the north.

All mountains are artifacts of two great antagonistic forces that shape the profile of the planet: orogeny (mountain building) and erosion. All mountain systems float like icebergs, with subterranean roots that thrust miles deep into the heavier rock of the earth's mantle. And all have been subjected, since their creation, to the weathering and leaching of implacable rains, and many to the surgery of ice. Yet individual mountain ranges are quite different from one another. Anyone who looks across Lake Champlain between the Adirondacks and the neighboring Green Mountains can perceive at a glance the difference in the character of their geologic forms. Many rocks of the Green Mountains are clearly stratified, laid down layer on layer in successive ages by sediments deposited in an ancient inland sea. Indeed it requires not too much searching on the lower slopes of the Green Mountains to find the remains of marine fossils and shells. But on the west side of Lake Champlain, the rocks are not stratified and they reveal no fossils, as we had noted on our climb down Giant.

Among the geologists closest to the intricate story of the Adirondacks' evolution is Yngvar W. Isachsen of the New York State Museum and Science Service in Albany. As he and others reconstruct the sequence of events, Adirondack geologic history began earlier than one billion, 100 million years ago—perhaps much earlier—when all of New York and the rest of Eastern North America lay under the waters of a geosyncline, a long narrow trough that contained a shallow sea. Into this primeval sea there drained sediments from a land mass to the west and an archipelago of volcanic islands to the east. No fish inhabited the waters; land animals would not evolve for another 700 million years.

As the millennia rolled on, the geosyncline, which stretched from

Labrador to the Gulf of Mexico, became gorged with sand, clay and other detritus from the mainland, while lavas and volcanic ash from the island arc added to the submarine mass and caused the trough to sag. Eventually the deposits, solidifying into sedimentary rock, reached a thickness of possibly seven or eight miles—and the sea floor sank. Then, perhaps owing to a collision of drifting continental land masses, lateral pressures came into play at right angles to the trough. This forced some of the accumulated sediment to buckle downward into the earth's mantle to a depth exceeding 20 miles, and also folded some of it upward to form mountains that may have been 20,000 or more feet high.

But no sooner had these newborn mountains thrust their young summits to the sky than the inevitable assault by water and gravity began to tear them down. Rocks were abraded into gravels, sands and clays, and swept down into a new geosynclinal trough encompassing most of Eastern North America. By middle to late Cambrian times—roughly 525 million years ago—the primeval Adirondacks had been worn down to a beveled highland. About 440 million years ago, a collision between the North American and European continental plates caused a new cycle of mountain building to begin, centered this time in New England, site of the thickest deposits, and locus of the most violent processes of folding and deformation. The Adirondack area to the west rose again in a pattern of ranges running from northeast to southwest —the pattern we know today. All five ranges of the Adirondacks are oriented in this direction, as are all the major lakes, which rest in valleys walled by scarps that follow fault lines created during the uplift.

For several hundreds of millions of years following this period of mountain building the geologic record is blank. The era must have been one of relative calm during which the earth's crust remained stable and the slow forces of erosion chiseled away at the reborn Adirondacks, furrowing their ridges and shoulders, incising their canyons, widening their valleys along the lower slopes. And then, perhaps a million years ago, came the climactic event of Adirondack history: the advent of the great ice sheets of the Pleistocene epoch.

At least four times stupendous invasions of ice moved down from the north, enveloping mountains, planing their pinnacles, grinding and polishing, scooping out lakes, stripping soil from Canada and depositing it in New York and New England, modifying the face of the region. Each time the glaciers moved forward with their massive tread, the land was depressed beneath their weight. Each time the ice receded, it left behind debris, forming drumlins (small hills) and moraines (ridges), damming valleys to create new lakes—and, as the ice melted, producing new rivers and streams.

The last ice sheet left the final imprint on the Adirondacks. Bearing away the soil, the glaciers laid bare the underlying bedrock, flayed by debris imbedded in the brutally abrasive glacial mass, and steepened the walls of V-shaped valleys and widened their floors, creating new U-shaped configurations. Later, when the climate warmed some 10,000 years ago, the ice retreated and the Atlantic Ocean invaded the depressed Saint Lawrence and Champlain valleys, bringing with it beach sand and sea shells. Then as the earth's crust rebounded in response to the melting of its burden of ice, the sea withdrew.

The rebound continues today. From time to time residents of the Adirondack region are aware of tremors that momentarily rock their houses gently—small earthquakes, never alarming, indicating simply that the earth's crust has not yet readjusted to the retreat of the last pressures of the ice. By the time such adjustments are made, a new set of circumstances—perhaps another ice age—will compel a further response from the environment. Thus, according to Isachsen, "The rocks are old, but the landscape is new."

And the landscape—composed of the underpinnings of vanished ranges—will repeatedly renew itself by crustal warping or upwelling of the earth's molten interior, and be destroyed repeatedly by the forces of erosion and gravity. As James Hutton, pioneer geologist, observed in a historic paper read before the Royal Society of Edinburgh in 1785, "We find no vestige of a beginning, no prospect of an end."

Evanescent though it may be in the grand sweep of time, the living Adirondack landscape of today has claimed the affection not only of a sparse and fiercely dedicated population of about 125,000 year-round residents, but also of some nine million seasonal visitors who come to ski in winter, fish for trout in spring, enjoy camping and water sports in the summer, and hunt ducks and deer in the fall. And then there are the climbers—of whom I am one.

To climbers from the Rockies and the high Sierra, the Adirondacks at first seem less like mountains than hills. Yet I have often met visitors from the Western states on Adirondack mountain trails; accustomed as they were to the open slopes of Colorado, Wyoming and Montana, they have expressed delight in the environmental variety experienced here as they ascended from deep, hardwood forests in the valleys, through the various transition zones of woodland to the alpine-like plants and naked rocks above timberline. I am talking now about trail walkers, whose numbers have increased enormously in recent years. For them, in an area of about 50 square miles in the northeast quadrant of the Adirondack Park, are clustered some 100 mountains that rise higher than 3,400 feet above sea level; of those, 46 are close to or higher than 4,000 feet. Ordered in five ranges, roughly parallel and about eight miles apart, separated by valleys and lakes but interconnected here and there by cross spurs and eccentric ridges, they are known as the High Peaks. Monarch among them is Mount Marcy, which in the summer of 1973 was climbed by an estimated 30,000 trail walkers.

For true rock climbers there are many abrupt and challenging precipices rising directly from lakes or valleys—most notably the great slide paths on Gothics, on Giant, on the east face of Marcy above Panther Gorge. Supreme among them is the 1,000-foot sheer cliff of Wallface above Indian Pass, whose glowering façade offers to practitioners of the rope and piton a degree of exposure found in few other mountain areas in the Eastern United States. And in winter, ice climbers can be seen on the steep slabs of Round Mountain above Chapel Pond. For the most part, these human dots on the peaks are not year-round Adirondack residents, but outsiders. They are downstaters and Canadians who form the constituency both of the Adirondack Mountain Club and of the elite group known as the Forty-Sixers: the conquerors of the 46 High Peaks.

Mountain climbing in the Adirondacks began in 1837 when a party under the leadership of Ebenezer Emmons, a professor at Williams College, engaged in a survey of the "Great Northern Wilderness." They took off from the McIntyre Iron Works at Tahawus, and headed up toward the Opalescent River, east branch of the Hudson, en route to the summit of Marcy. Guiding the party was John Cheney, the first of a band of local guides during the late 19th Century. After camping overnight at Lake Colden, the Emmons-Cheney group climbed painfully upward through difficult terrain overgrown with dwarf spruce and balsam fir, whose interwoven branches can be—as I well know—almost impenetrable. They eventually reached the clear summit of the mountain, tufted only with mosses and small plants. Emmons named the peak Mount Marcy in honor of the governor of New York state, William Learned Marcy. Cheney's description of the moment as he stood at the highest point of New York state, is one of the most powerful expressions of affection for these mountains ever written:

"It makes a man feel what it is to have all creation placed beneath

The central peaks of the main range,
backbone of the Adirondack massif,
dominate the horizon above the
changing foliage on the north shore of
Upper Ausable Lake. Nearby at left,
the scarred dome of Basin, ninth highest
in the range, shades the quiet waters.
Over its shoulder, Saddleback
rises above snow-dusted ridges at left
center. At right, the naked façade of
Gothics, whose slides suggest gigantic
cathedral windows, soars to the sky.

his feet. There are woods there which it would take a lifetime to hunt over; mountains that seem shouldering each other, to boost the one whereon you stand up and away, heaven knows where. Thousands of little lakes are let in among them, so bright and clean that you would like to keep a canoe on each of them. Old Champlain, though 50 miles off, glistens below you like a strip of white birch bark, when slicked up by the moon on a frosty night; and the Green Mountains of Vermont beyond it fade and fade away, till they disappear as gradually as a cold scent when the dew rises."

Though John Cheney, who led Emmons to the heights, was one of the first Adirondack guides of record, the most famous was Orson Schofield Phelps—"Old Mountain Phelps." A native Vermonter, Phelps first came to the Adirondacks about 1830 with his father, a surveyor. Old Mountain was a philosopher, a poet and an eccentric. "Soap is a thing," he said, "that I hain't no kinder use for." As for water, he proclaimed, "I don't believe in this etarnal sozzlin'!" What he did believe in was the beauty and excitement of a mountaintop and, unlike other early Adirondack guides who contented themselves with providing food and portages for hunters and anglers, he had an urge to inspire his clients with the feeling of "Heaven-up-h'istedness," such as could be obtained only on the summit of a high peak. He got to the top of dozens of them and climbed Mount Marcy (which he always pronounced *Mercy*) hundreds of times, and from every direction. And it was he who bestowed its descriptive name on the nearby peak, Haystack—because, he said, it resembled "a great stack of rock," shaped like a stack of hay.

Orson Phelps, who died at the age of 87 in 1905, was almost the last of the Adirondack mountain guides. Few need them today; their function is performed by well-marked trails, with hostels and lean-tos maintained by the Adirondack Mountain Club, the Adirondack Trail Improvement Society and the New York State Department of Environmental Conservation. In short, the guides gave way to an organized system of wilderness use—a park. The man most responsible for creating within the Adirondacks the largest park in the United States was some 30 years younger than Old Mountain Phelps, but no less dedicated, no less passionate a mountaineer.

Verplanck Colvin, born in 1847, was the son of a wealthy Albany lawyer, Andrew Colvin, who hoped that his only son would follow him into law. But by the time he was 18, Verplanck Colvin was committing himself in a quite different direction, climbing in the Adirondacks and making maps for his own amusement. He abandoned the idea of a legal career, went west, climbed for a while in the Rockies, then returned to Albany and Adirondack country, the love of his life. When he was barely of age, Colvin began to lobby for the creation of an Adirondack park or timber preserve, predicting a time when New York City would need a subsidiary source of water supply. He also argued that the Adirondack area had been inadequately explored, mapped and surveyed, and proposed a new system of surveying by theodolite, transit and barometer for which he was willing to underwrite expenses and commit himself to a labor that would involve thousands of observations and enormous physical effort over many years. His energy and enthusiasm impressed the legislature, and in 1872 a commission on state parks was created and a topographical survey approved. Colvin was appointed superintendent of the survey at a salary of $2,500 a year.

Colvin could not have cared less about the salary. He spent the next 28 years in the Adirondacks as the state surveyor, publishing a variety of reports about his work, many of which read like tales from a true-adventure magazine. Again and again Colvin recounts stories of descending icy cliffs at midnight, or of being caught by storms on mountaintops without food, or of being attacked by a panther or wolves. He was precise and painstaking, and a slave driver to his assistants. The data he secured proved invaluable. Colvin knew the Adirondacks as did no other man, and in the course of his work he drew public attention to the area as a reservoir of priceless natural resources for New York state. These efforts led to the establishment of the Adirondack Forest Preserve in 1885 and of the Adirondack Park in 1892.

Among Colvin's many exploring achievements perhaps the most notable was discovering and naming the highest headwater of the Hudson River in 1872. With companions he had been exploring the slopes of Marcy, plunging through dense thickets of dwarf balsam, traversing precipitous ledges, leaping and sliding over slippery rocks. An excerpt from a Colvin report tells what happened next: "Suddenly, before us, through the trees gleamed a sheet of water, and we shouted our 'hurrah!' It was the lake, and [it] flowed, not to the Ausable and St. Lawrence, but to the Hudson, the loftiest lake spring of our haughty river! But how wild and desolate this spot! There is no mark of ax, no barked tree, nor blackened remnants of fire; not a severed twig, nor a human footprint. . . . And now, skirting the shores, we seek the inlet, and find that the numerous subterranean streams from different directions feed its waters. The spring rills which feed these streams come from far up on the sides of the . . . mountains, the water dripping from the crest of Marcy. First seen as we then saw it . . . dripping with the moisture of the heavens, it seemed, in its minuteness and its prettiness, a veritable Tear-of-the-Clouds, the summit water as I named it."

At this very spot, 29 years later, Vice President Theodore Roosevelt was enjoying a picnic lunch, following an ascent of Mount Marcy. Roosevelt's vacation was far from carefree: President William McKinley, who had been shot by an anarchist in Buffalo, was still in the hands of the doctors. The attack on McKinley had taken place on September 6, 1901, and Vice President Roosevelt had hastened to Buffalo, where he remained until he was told the President was out of danger. Reassured, T.R. went to join his family, which had preceded him to the Tahawus Club southwest of Mount Marcy.

Teddy Roosevelt was no stranger to the Adirondacks. As a boy, in the 1870s, he had spent three summers in the Saint Regis Lakes area, and there became a premier ornithologist. He was, indeed, the first to report in detail on Adirondack bird life; and, remarkably enough, he prepared a catalogue listing 97 different species. (More recent observers have cited about 165.)

As a New Yorker, Roosevelt had been determined to climb what Emmons had discovered 64 years earlier to be the highest mountain in New York state. And despite bad weather, he did so. After spending the night at Lake Colden, he and his party had ascended the Opalescent River-Feldspar Brook Trail to the summit of Marcy, which they reached at about noon on Friday, September 13. Finding themselves surrounded by clouds and drizzling rain, they remained only 15 minutes. They then descended over the steep rock ledges leading down to Lake Tear of the Clouds. There, while resting and eating their lunch, they suddenly perceived a man hurrying from the woods below. The courier handed T.R. a telegram informing him that President McKinley was dying. This was at 2 p.m.

The party ran down the mountain—no easy task even for a guide who knows the Feldspar Brook Trail—and reached the Tahawus Club at 5:15. Since there was no further word, Roosevelt decided to spend the night; dusk was falling. But at 11 p.m. another message arrived, reporting McKinley's condition as dire. At this, Roosevelt insisted on starting immediately for Buffalo. The railhead at North Creek lay 40 miles to the south. But the roads were rough and treacherous, especially on a dark and misty night.

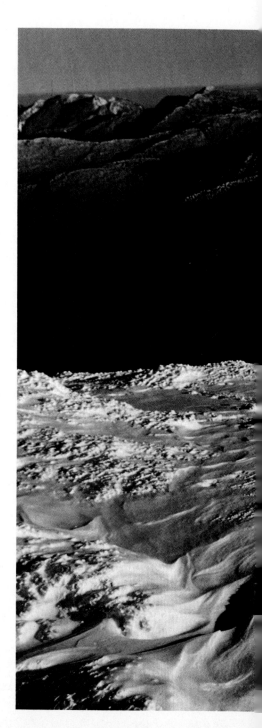

Tallest of the High Peaks and hub of the area, Mount Marcy thrusts its snowy summit to the sky in this view from Algonquin Peak.

When his friends urged him to delay his departure until daylight, Roosevelt asked for a lantern and said he would go afoot. His threat induced one of the guides to volunteer as a driver—and thus began Teddy Roosevelt's famous midnight drive, a journey made in three relays, with T.R. jumping from one buckboard to another. At 4:46 a.m. he alighted at the North Creek station, where a special train was waiting, and an aide informed him that he was now President of the United States. The last driver of the storied midnight relay was an Adirondacker named Mike Cronin, who subsequently became a kind of national hero. A legend grew up that Cronin, besieged by journalists and others who asked him for the worn-down shoes of his famous team of black midnight racers as souvenirs of a historic event, eventually sold or gave away more than 400 horseshoes.

At the time of Roosevelt's journey, the ascent of Mount Marcy was still something of an adventure. The first climbers to conquer all 46 of the High Peaks, including Marcy of course, were brothers named Robert and George Marshall and their guide, Herbert Clark. As boys vacationing at their family's camp on Lower Saranac Lake, the Marshalls gazed south toward the challenge of blue rolling ranges under the summer sky. They began climbing while still in their teens and on June 10, 1925, completed their self-appointed rounds. Inspired by their experience, both Marshalls subsequently devoted much of their time to conservationist causes. One unique by-product of their climbing days was an esthetic evaluation of the High Peaks according to the view from their summits. Thus, in the Marshalls' rating list, Mount Marcy, No. 1 in height, ranks only eighth as a view point, doubtless because of the undifferentiated quality of the panorama it affords. They ranked Haystack (No. 3 in height) No. 1 for its view (pages 68-69)—a judgment few who have ever scaled it would dispute.

Today the roll of Forty-Sixers has grown to almost a thousand —among them one who earned his emblem at the age of six, and another who won his at the age of 70. I must confess that I am not a member. I have climbed all the best and loveliest mountains and returned to my favorites many times; I can claim more than half. Those I have passed by are trailless and wooded on top, and while I acknowledge the pleasure of a scramble up a forested mountainside, I tend to crave the big prize, the spiritual sense of what Old Mountain Phelps called Heaven-up-h'istedness. My friend Bill Verner, curator of the Adirondack Museum, thinks I overemphasize the importance of the view from the top. "Personally," he once told me, "I have had some of my best and most intriguing mountain experiences in such thick fog at high elevations that you couldn't see your hand in front of you."

Be that as it may, I have always preferred open mountains that offer not only summit views but sections of trail with sudden, surprising windows along the way. There is, for example, the exciting trail that runs along the crest of the main range from Marcy to Gothics, dipping down into cols bristling with small conifers, then soaring steeply again to naked rock. I think too of the Trap Dike on Colden and the great slide on McComb—open rock all the way. Neither of these climbs requires alpine equipment. But near the approach to the top of McComb the grade steepens to a point where special gear almost seems necessary: only the grip of friction soles preserves the climber from an unstoppable glissade to the rocks more than 2,000 feet below.

One need not even climb, however, to enjoy the sights and splendors of the High Peaks. For it is almost true, as a native axiom claims, that every Adirondack mountain has its own lake. So from lakeshore, guide boat or canoe, beauty can be won by looking up to the sky. No sight transcends, I think, the view from the south shore of Upper Ausable Lake, looking toward the heart of the main range. Here, framed in a proscenium of ridges, three great mountains—Basin, Saddleback and Gothics—leap upward dramatically in a jagged, dizzying cyclorama of multicolored forest and gray rock. It is hard to reach this observation point, for Upper Ausable Lake lies deep in the wilderness and can be attained only by a journey of many miles on foot and by boat.

Old Mountain Phelps cherished this sanctuary and, in a strange way, protected it. He once led the writer Charles Dudley Warner and some friends here and, after allowing them a few moments of rapture, announced they would now cross the lake and camp on the other side. They protested, arguing that they wished to see the sun set and rise on this glorious scene. But Phelps was adamant, for he was temperate in his intake of beauty and imbibed it sparingly, as a connoisseur sips rare wine. When his party continued to press him to set up camp where they were, Phelps finally exploded. "Waal now," he exclaimed, "them Gothics ain't the kinder scenery yer want ter *hog down!*"

Secret Sources of the Hudson

PHOTOGRAPHS BY DAN BUDNIK

The Hudson, its wide mouth the locus of the world's largest seaport, is paradoxically a river that few men have seen in its entirety. From the time of Henry Hudson's first voyage halfway up the river in 1609—blocked by unnavigable shoals, he could sail no farther than the present site of Albany—two centuries passed before the source of the stream was discovered. And even on present-day maps, the actual wellspring of the river is not readily recognizable. For the stream that bears the name Hudson River emanates from Henderson Lake (page 94), which actually lies more than six miles below the Hudson's true headwaters (right). The runoff from this diminutive lake rushes through a succession of streams until it becomes part of the main river downstream from Henderson.

Though tens of millions have come to know the Hudson's lower course —New York harbor itself, the basalt rampart of the Palisades, the broad sweep of the Tappan Zee, the highlands above West Point, the meeting with the Mohawk—the river's sources kept their secret until barely a century ago. Their discoverer was Verplanck Colvin, an official surveyor for New York state, who spent 28

years completing the first accurate topographic study of the Adirondacks. In 1872, skirting the slopes of Mount Marcy with his team of assistants, Colvin burst through a curtain of spruce, balsam and white cedar, and saw the glitter of a pond, a true glacial tarn, nestled in the col between Marcy and its neighbor, Mount Skylight. Aware that he had made a momentous discovery, Colvin shared his excitement when composing his official report to the New York State Legislature: "Far above the chilly waters of Lake Avalanche, at an elevation of 4,293 feet . . . is a minute, unpretending tear of the clouds . . . a lovely pool shivering in the breezes of the mountains, and sending its limpid surplus through Feldspar Brook and to the Opalescent River, the wellspring of the Hudson." The legislators, moved by Colvin's eloquence, adopted his phrase "tear of the clouds" as the little lake's official name.

The lake and surrounding forests that Colvin saw remain essentially untouched today. And of the 161 miles traveled by the Hudson between Lake Tear and the river's confluence with the Mohawk, more than half still lies in wilderness, remote, roadless, seldom seen.

A gleaming dot in the forest, Lake Tear of the Clouds, highest source of the Hudson River, lies cradled in a col below the summit of Mount Marcy (right foreground). Beyond the tiny lake, looking due west, stand the ragged MacIntyre Mountains (far right) and the Santanoni Range (top left).

A thin ribbon of cold mountain water, the Hudson's first flow winds through the marsh at Lake Tear's outlet to feed Feldspar Brook.

A Long Seaward Journey Begins at Lake Tear

Jewel-like though it still appears from a distance, at close range Lake Tear is vanishing. Since Colvin's find, Lake Tear has evolved, as all ponds do, along the way to becoming dry land. With every heavy rain and spring thaw, silt and plant debris wash down from the slopes of Marcy and Skylight into the shallow basin. Each year reeds and grasses inch farther out from shore. In time plants will carpet the surface and the lake will become a marsh.

But today the Hudson's source waters still trickle through the outlet at the west end of the lake. Thence, channeled into the steep trough of Feldspar Brook, they accelerate as they tumble down the side of Marcy, dropping almost 1,000 feet in little more than a mile. No fish inhabit Feldspar Brook: its grade is too steep, the humus too acid and the spring runoff too violent to sustain the aquatic insect life on which brook trout depend.

At an elevation of 3,319 feet, Feldspar dives into the Opalescent River (overleaf), which has wound down from Marcy. Incorporating Feldspar's flow, the Opalescent plunges through canyons and chasms, over falls and rapids. Its clear waters strike cold fire—green, gold and blue —from the iridescent labradorite rocks that give the stream its name. Some 10 miles southeast of Lake Tear and 2,543 feet lower, the Opalescent meets a modest bit of water called the Hudson River.

Surging by a mossy boulder, Feldspar Brook takes refreshment from a melting June snow.

A nameless mountain rivulet tumbles down the tangled slopes of Mount Colden to join the Opalescent River. The trees and branches sprawled on the banks are relics of a hurricane that devastated the Adirondacks in 1950.

The Opalescent River gains strength as it joins Feldspar Brook (lower left). Here the river is strewn with glacial erratics—boulders dropped during the ice age and differing in composition from the rock on which they lie.

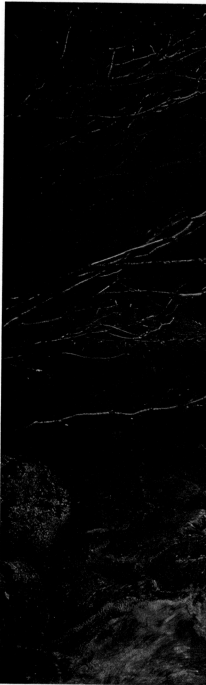

*Still some 300 miles from the sea,
the Opalescent River roars through The
Flume, a deep gorge with nearly
vertical walls rising above tiered falls
and rapids. Beyond this wild raceway
the Opalescent widens and then
meanders gently to its junction with
the Hudson six miles downstream.*

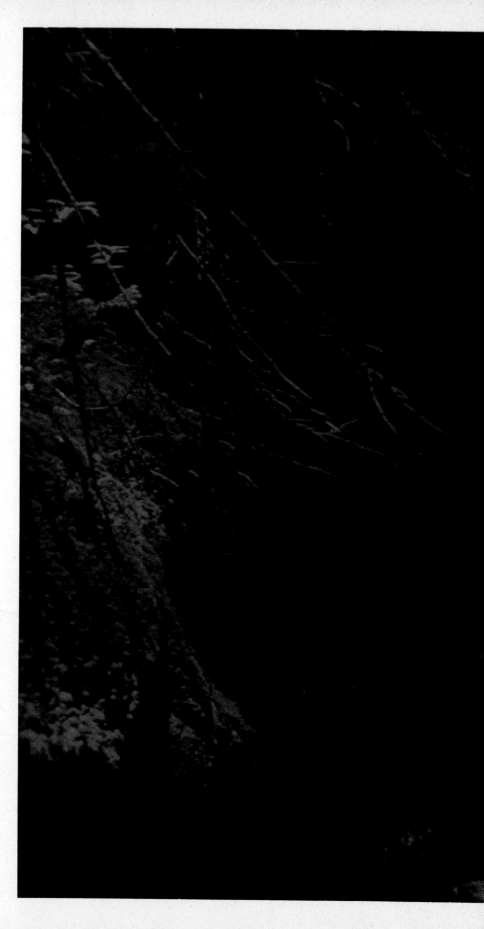

The nominal source of the Hudson, mile-long Henderson Lake draws its water from spring-fed brooks high in the surrounding hills.

A Quiet Send-off for the Main Stream

Long-standing ignorance of the actual source of the Hudson accounts for the fact that the name makes its northernmost appearance on maps at the outlet of Henderson Lake *(left)*. A few miles downstream from Henderson the young Hudson, until then a narrow and relatively shallow brook, broadens into Sanford Lake near the old iron-mining settlement of Adirondac; the river then meanders indecisively to the town of Newcomb, where it straightens out and heads 12 miles southwest. There it joins the Indian River, and turns 90° to the southeast, hurtling into the wildest leg of its long journey to the sea—the passage through Hudson Gorge. Locked between vertical cliffs towering in places more than 800 feet high, the river foams over fierce rapids, broken at intervals by deep trout pools. The climax of the gorge is reached at the Harris Rift, where the Hudson cascades through a 200-yard stretch known as Big Nasty Rapids. In former days, many loggers lost their lives here clearing the river of jams during the annual spring drives; today canoeists compete each spring, pitting their skills in white-water races. A few miles below the rift, the Hudson leaves the wilderness and the Adirondacks, and resumes a gentler aspect, slipping tranquilly down to Albany between fields and meadows, through glassy lakes where on windless days fishermen troll silently for bass and pike.

As a streamlet emerging from Henderson Lake, the Hudson can be crossed in a stride.

Below Henderson Lake, the young Hudson widens to form Sanford Lake, seen here looking north toward Wallface Mountain and the jagged peaks of the MacIntyre Mountains in the background. Directly below the river's exit from the lake, the Hudson is joined by the Opalescent.

Entering the Hudson Gorge some 25 miles downstream from Sanford Lake, the river flows beneath Blue Ledge, a spectacular marble rock face rising up to 400 feet, its blue tint caused by a number of mineral impurities.

As the sun rises above the Hudson Gorge, cool air from the first September frost forms mist over the warmer waters of the moving current. Downstream from this relatively quiet stretch, the river's flow speeds up as the Hudson plunges headlong into the rapids of Harris Rift.

In Harris Rift, wildest stretch of the upper Hudson, a series of boulder-studded rapids churns the river into a maelstrom. The water rushes

for a mile through Hudson Gorge; in places cataracts alternate with narrow chutes that abruptly hurl the current from side to side.

4/ The Deep Woods

…a pillared shade
High overarched, and echoing walks between.

JOHN MILTON/ *PARADISE LOST*

In the Adirondacks the first days of June are the best of times and the worst of times. Overhead the tender green of the late-leafing mountain maples, beeches and white birches begins to interweave with the darker strands of the conifers. Underfoot the white constellations of the starflower, the spume of the foamflower and the vessel of the pink lady's-slipper enliven the forest floor. Bird voices float on the air—the songs of warblers and finches, and the infinitely plaintive flute call of the white-throated sparrow. But amid the beauty and the music there hovers a silent and most malignant foe. I have known it as long as I have known the Adirondacks, but familiarity with this adversary does not confer any protection against it—as I discovered once again on a recent June walk in the woods.

"This is where we start," said Greenleaf Chase, chief biologist of the Adirondack Park Agency, pulling his car off to the right of New York State Highway 3, which runs southwest from Saranac Lake to Tupper Lake, virtually dead center of the Adirondack region. "It's not a marked trail. As a matter of fact it's not really a human trail. It happens to be a deer runway, and I'd be grateful if you didn't locate it too specifically in what you write. I happen to be very fond of it, and I'd like to keep it to myself—that is, for me and the deer."

We climbed a bank on the south side of the road, scrambled through some underbrush, and found ourselves on the narrow runway, well trodden and clearly identified by many clusters of deer pellets. The trail paralleled a brook bed and was overhung with hemlock. Within minutes the sound of traffic on the highway had faded into silence.

Ferns were everywhere—oak fern, sensitive fern, ostrich fern and wood fern, which provides summer and autumn forage for the deer. And there was other forage: hobblebush, wood honeysuckle and a striped, shrubby tree known as moose maple. All are crucial to the deer that cluster here for protection in winter. The overarching conifers provide shelter against the boreal winds. The seedlings of hardwoods and softwoods rising a few inches above the snow—snow kept down a bit by the awning of evergreens above—supply sustenance during the harsh Adirondack winter, which may last from November till May.

"I wanted you to take this particular walk," Greenie said, "because it contains in this one forest rectangle—a tract of about 20 square miles in the very center of the park—just about every variety of woodland habitat you'll find in the entire Adirondack forest. We'll go about four miles in and four miles out in an oval pattern. We'll see hardwood groves, spruce, hemlock and fir stands, cedar swamps, bogs and a big wetland created by beavers. The average elevation of this tract—with a few ups and downs—is about eighteen hundred feet."

I knew from long experience in the High Peaks area the variations of forest zones as they are defined by altitude. In low wetlands, softwoods like spruce and balsam fir dominate. Maple, yellow birch and the other hardwoods, which cannot tolerate an overabundance of moisture, prevail on the well-drained middle zone of the mountain slopes, up to an altitude of 2,500 feet. Between 2,500 feet and 4,200 feet, where the soil becomes thinner and the wind stronger, the maple, yellow birch, ash, beech and cherry—all of which have deep taproots—cannot survive. At this point the shallow and flat-rooted fir and red spruce largely take over again, predominating from 4,200 feet to 4,700 feet. Finally, at about 4,700 feet the red spruce surrender to the bitter environment, leaving only such hardy species as black spruce, balsam fir, and diminutive mountain ash and willow just below timberline, which on the High Peaks occurs at about 4,900 feet.

But now we were not climbing, although the deer runway had its undulations. In our first hour of walking we found ourselves for the most part amid hardwoods on the ridge above the brook; below us on our right we could see the hemlock and spruce that provided a snow umbrella for the winter habitat of the deer. Many maples and yellow birches towered 80 feet high or more, and I asked Greenie Chase if he was certain this could not be called primeval forest. Or perhaps virgin?

"Those are vague terms," he said. "Some of these trees, like that whopper of a maple over there, must be crowding two hundred years, maybe two hundred and fifty. But does that make it virgin? I'd describe it as first-growth climax. Remember that the great forests of the 16th and 17th centuries were basically white pine, the great white pine, intermingled with hemlock and giant red spruce, many of them seven feet around at the base. It was only after the primeval pines and spruce were cut down that the hardwoods moved in."

I knew that the first destruction of the Adirondack forest had begun with the colonization by the French of the Saint Lawrence River Valley in the 17th and 18th centuries, when voyageurs made frequent sorties down the Richelieu River to Lake Champlain. By the latter part of the 18th Century the French colonists had virtually denuded Lake Champlain's shores of their majestic pines, floating them to the Saint Lawrence for transshipment to the royal navy. Farther south the British were busy cutting the towering conifers around Ticonderoga for their own navy. More than likely, many of the British and French ships that fought one another at Trafalgar in 1805 were equipped with masts and spars and planking from the Adirondack woods.

The sorry fact is that by 1800 much of·the giant white pine along the shores of Lake Champlain and Lake George—the most easily accessible areas of the great Adirondack forest—was gone. And by 1850 white pine was an endangered species in the Adirondacks. Not many years thereafter the red spruce followed into the mills of the timber industry—colossal trees, often towering more than 100 feet, with diameters of two feet or more and a ring count of more than 200 years.

But not for shipbuilding or homebuilding. In 1867 it was discovered that the long spruce fibers were the best raw material for paper pulp. The slaughter of red spruce was relentless—at least until 1885, when the state legislature created the Forest Preserve and enacted the famous and still controversial "forever wild" provision, which preserved the Adirondack wilderness and is now perpetuated in the state constitution.

"Look here," said Greenie Chase. "Some of the early spring flowers have gone. These are trillium leaves, but the blossoms have gone. Here's a false lily of the valley. Here's a wood honeysuckle. And this is a pretty wood sorrel—its leaves are kind of like a shamrock's."

At this moment, as I bent over to admire the graceful green geometry of the ground plants in the shade of a maple grove, the silent and ma-

In the heart of a cedar swamp near the village of Moriah, showy lady's-slippers glorify the early summer with their orchid blossoms.

lignant foe struck. It was the Adirondack blackfly, pestilential foe of man and deer in these forests. Shaped like the familiar housefly, but less than a quarter the size, the blackfly carries a venom that produces a swelling that may last for two weeks and can make allergic persons ill. The fly is the torment of the trout fisherman, because it breeds and hatches in cool running streams. And it can torture the deer to a point where their only recourse is to plunge into a lake. Fortunately the season of the Adirondack blackfly is brief. It emerges from the larval stage in early June and infests the woods only until mid-July.

Remembering an experience I had as a boy on a camping trip in the High Peaks when I woke up one morning with both eyes closed by blackfly bites on my eyelids, I had been somewhat hesitant about venturing into the woods in June. I did, however, want to explore this special territory of Greenie's, so I smeared myself with two brands of well-known insect repellent. However, when I suddenly felt blood streaming from a puncture somewhere behind my right ear, and began to suffer the intolerable itch, I knew that I had been hit. I asked Greenie what kind of blackfly repellent he considered the best.

"A switch," he said. I smeared myself with some more goo. "The trouble with that stuff is that it doesn't always keep the blackflies away, but it sure keeps people away."

We began moving now into a zone of mixed forest, with some hemlock and spruce intermingling with the hardwoods.

"The reason the Adirondack forests are now mostly hardwoods," Greenie said, "is that the hardwoods are more aggressive on logged-over lands. One of the few remaining stands of virgin pine is in the Pack Forest at Warrensburg. But we'll see one old friend of mine further on."

He went on to point out that another powerful influence on the character of the Adirondacks had been a series of forest fires, the most dreadful in 1903. An unusually dry winter in 1902-1903 had reduced the annual blanket of snow to several inches below the average of the preceding decade. The dry winter was followed by a dry spring—only two inches of rain early in April and almost none the rest of the month. In May the rainfall was only two tenths of an inch, the lowest ever recorded for the month.

The ruthless harvesters of timber had left in their wake top branches and so-called trash trees, which lay on the cutover lands, drying in the sun like so much tinder. Throughout the Adirondack forest, the cutover clearings lay susceptible to every spark left by a smoker or camper, a farmer or berrypicker.

Nor were these the only dangers. Fishermen were building camp-fires and smudge fires to ward off insects. The locomotives of the New York Central and the Delaware and Hudson Railroad, as well as those of the lumber-company railroads, casually discharged cinders from their stacks, unimpeded that year by the spark arresters later required by New York state law. On May 5, 1903, an excursion train hauled by two locomotives set almost continuous fires for 10 miles.

Inevitably, the flames erupted out of control. A brush-clearing fire set by a farmer near Lake Placid smoldered for weeks. Then, suddenly, fanned to a blaze by high winds, it swept eight miles through the woods in two and a half hours. The flames leaped from the leaves at one tree-top to those at another in a classic crown blaze—the most difficult to fight. Literally thousands of smaller fires burst forth everywhere, and they too were almost impossible to bring under control. Camp buildings in the Nehasane Preserve, where 12,000 acres went up, were saved only when fire engines were rushed in by railway from Herkimer and Ilion, 75 and 100 miles away. A suffocating blanket of smoke lay everywhere; residents in the area could sleep only by lying on the floors of their houses and cabins.

Between April 20 and June 8 of 1903, more than 600,000 acres of timberland burned. The total economic loss was estimated at $3.5 million. The future loss in young growth, soil, seed source and wildlife was incalculable. The fires killed every tree on 17,000 acres around Keene and Elizabethtown. But the biggest single loss of all was the total destruction of 40,000 acres on the estate of William Rockefeller, brother of John D. Rockefeller Sr.

And here a sinister note appeared—arson. The rapid increase in the number and extent of private estates and game preserves in the Adirondacks, and the resulting decrease in the areas open to free hunting and fishing by local residents, created bitter feelings toward the rich men from downstate who had bought up large tracts of land and had them patrolled by shotgun-toting guards. So in the spring of 1903, a number of these private preserves burned.

Now the morning was advancing. The sun rose higher and I noticed that the blackflies were no longer attacking as savagely as before. Greenie explained that this could be expected: the flies are most active in the cool, humid hours of the morning and evening; in the hot, dry hours of midday they retreat to shelter under plant growth. Mercifully, then, we were able to forget them for a while.

"In talking about the evolution of the Adirondack woodlands," Greenie said, "you've got to remember that a forest is vulnerable to a lot of things. In addition to the fires and the ruthless lumbering that changed the character of the forest, there's disease—not just the familiar Dutch elm disease, but beech canker and others.

"Wind also hurts. The greatest blowdown in history took place in the fall of 1950, when a hurricane took not just thousands but millions of the grandest trees in the park.

"There's another enemy of the forest that's been important in recent years—the automobile. To keep the roads open in winter the local town and county highway departments spread quantities of sand mixed with salt. After a thaw, the salt runs off into the woods, seeps into the soil and poisons many trees, especially the pines. Drive anywhere in the park and you'll come to stretches where the roads are lined with batches of dead pines."

As a result of these various factors induced by man and nature, the hardwood beeches, birches and maples dominate the Adirondack Park from the High Peaks in the east to the Lake Country in the west, constituting more than 50 per cent of the forest cover. The once-predominant pines account for less than 10 per cent.

For all the changes in the forest's character, as Greenie and I walked deeper into the woods I felt the sense of magic that Verplanck Colvin, the first Adirondack surveyor, experienced in 1879: "The Adirondack wilderness . . . is a mystery even to those who have crossed and recrossed it by boats along its avenues—the lakes; and on foot through its vast and silent recesses. . . . Though the woodsman may pass his lifetime in some section of the wilderness, it is still a mystery to him [as he] emerges at length from its darkness to the daylight of its clearings."

The feeling of wonder deepened as Greenie and I progressed past brooklets, fallen trees, random pools, mosses, new growth, catching through occasional windows in the green rampart of the trees a distant view of mountains. From time to time Greenie called my attention to ground plants and shrubs—the sharp-leaved hepatica with its trilobed foliage, maidenhair fern, viburnum, a profusion of maple seedlings that had somehow escaped the deer, and squirrel corn, a plant that justifies its name only when you pluck it, thereby disclosing two small orange tubers that resemble kernels of corn concealed at its roots.

Shortly thereafter we came upon a phenomenon I first discovered in the writings of the great 19th Century historian Francis Parkman: "Fall-

Behaving remarkably like water-browsing moose, three whitetail does and a fawn wade in Deer Pond, near Newcomb. During early summer, deer often come to the lake to feed on water shield, an aquatic plant, sometimes swimming out into deeper waters to munch on it. Wildlife biologists theorize that the deer seek out water shield for its high concentration of sodium, a nutrient that is rare in terrestrial plants in spring and summer.

en trunks [that], bent in the impotence of rotteness . . . lie outstretched over knoll and hollow . . . while around, and on and through them, springs the young growth that battens on their decay—the forest devouring its own dead." Growing out of an old, prostrate log, a six-inch hemlock seedling rose above a cover of green moss that had mantled the dead tree like a funereal shroud. "This is a fairly common sight," Greenie said. "It's very difficult for young seedlings to get through the ground cover of leaves, especially during a dry spring or summer. But old fallen logs with a moss cover provide good nursery sites. Big growing trees take moisture out of the soil, so it's tough for seedlings to get going in their first year. But there is moisture in moss and moisture in a rotting log, so this is a fine place for a hemlock to begin."

As noon approached, I was beginning to feel a bit hungry and I asked Greenie whether he had a picnic site in mind. We had walked about three miles in from the road, still paralleling the stream below. The day was hot and I had a couple of cans of well-insulated beer in my knapsack. All of a sudden Greenie stopped and pointed to a mound of what appeared to be black mud beside the runway.

"That," he said, "is a bear dropping."

"How can you tell it's a bear dropping?"

"I've seen them many times. The reason it's so black is that at this time of year the bear eats a lot of roots and in digging for roots and ingesting them he gets a lot of just plain black dirt. Anyway, look there."

He pointed at a tree with a section of bark stripped from its trunk about five feet above the ground. Sap was oozing out. "That's his blaze," Greenie added. "See the teeth marks. He does it with his teeth, not his claws. He took a bite, which means this is his territory, keep off."

"What if we meet him and he objects to our using his trail?" I asked.

"The Adirondack bear is one of the shyest creatures on earth. If he senses us, he'll head in the opposite direction. The only time an Adirondack black bear can be dangerous is when it's cornered."

A moment later we came to a huge boulder covered with moss. It was just noon, and we sat on the edge of a needled bank, looking down on the stream below, and produced our sandwiches and beer. For a while we lunched in silence, listening to the birds in the canopy overhead —the rather harsh mewing notes of the red-eyed vireo (whose repetitious vocalization has led some ornithologists to nickname it The Preacher) and the whistling warble of the rose-breasted grosbeak.

As we sat there, Greenie reflected on the unhappy life of the white-tailed deer, the most abundant large mammal in the Adirondack forest. "Let's take the seasons in turn," he said. "Start with winter. As the snows fall, the deer suffer from lots of problems—they suffer from cold, just as we do, and they don't hole up in dens like bears. And though we speak of our climatic zone as temperate, Adirondack temperatures are seldom temperate. They may range from the 90s in the summer to 60 below in the winter. The deer's mobility is impaired because snows may accumulate to a height of five or six feet. Many deer simply get stuck in the snow and die of cold and starvation.

"Then there's the problem of food. In summer the deer graze on grasses and tree sprouts, and on fiddlehead ferns and goldenrod. In the autumn they turn to the nut crop, beech nuts mostly, because few acorns are available north of Lake George. In winter they switch from grazing to browsing, which means nibbling at whatever soft woody vegetation may appear above the snow—cedar, hemlock, ash and maple." (On the other hand, deer dislike beech, except for the nuts, and eat spruce only as a last resort.)

"Then the spring thaws come, the insects emerge, and as the food situation improves, the deer are plagued constantly by stinging insects, chiefly the blackfly and the deerfly, which not only draws blood but makes a deep incision in the flesh. As the insects wane in autumn, the hunting season begins. And so with an abundance of food and the torment of insects removed, the deer then face men's guns. When the hunting season ends, winter sets in and the whole cycle begins again. I'd hate to lead the life of an Adirondack deer."

I said that I thought deer were beautiful animals and that I could never bring myself to kill one. Greenie sympathized, but added that control of the deer population was important to the balance of the Adirondack forest. The natural predators—wolves and panthers, for example—are long gone from the Adirondacks, he pointed out, and the deer do proliferate, despite their difficulties. "If hunting were forbidden," Greenie said, "and the deer multiplied uncontrolled, they'd be starving to death all over the forest. In the process they'd eat most of the hemlock and maple and ash. We'd have mostly beech and spruce."

We finished our sandwiches and beer, and carefully stuffed the sandwich wrappings and the empty cans in our parachute-cloth knapsacks. "You've seen the signs at the start of many of the Adirondack trails," Greenie said. "They read: 'You carried it in. Carry it out.' But you'd be amazed at how many people feel that the first rule of environmental conservation is 'Heave the beer bottle as far as you can.'"

As we resumed our course, in a generally westerly direction, Greenie explained that soon we would reach the wet area created by beavers.

"At first I kind of resented those beavers," Greenie said. "I was annoyed because they flooded out my trail, and they flooded out a lot of big timber. But I forgave them. They create open spaces that attract deer, raccoons, bear, frogs and little creatures like the water shrews, moles, voles and mice. They let sunlight in, seeds sprout, berries grow. There's a rush of vegetation, and you get ferns, sedges, grasses and a lot of insects—these open glades attract a variety of birds."

We were indeed getting into wet ground—a white-cedar swamp, with islands of sphagnum moss like patches of green sponge. At one point we passed a dead black-ash tree with a ruby-throated hummingbird perched on it. A little farther on we came to a purple bed of violets. And then a footprint, pad and claws.

"I guess we're on the right trail," Greenie said. "There's our bear's track. This white-cedar thicket, by the way, is a perfect deer yard for winter, an ancient glacial lake bottom, centuries old, filled in by cedars, dammed up by beavers, a typical Adirondack swamp where the deer can take refuge in winter."

I was not too happy at the moment because as I leaped from island to island of sphagnum moss I sank into water over my boot tops. And the insects were beginning to attack again. Then we crossed a lovely little trout stream onto firmer land.

"Now," said Greenie, "I want you to meet that old friend of mine. Old Joe, I call him." He pointed to an enormous white pine, towering through the forest canopy and at least four feet in diameter at the base. "I don't know how it escaped the loggers in the last century. But there he stands, Old Joe. He stands alone because squirrels can control the destiny of a single tree. If you have only one tree they take most of the cones and there's little chance of more trees sprouting."

The afternoon was wearing on now, and we began to swing back toward the highway, through wet lands and dry lands, through groves of hemlock, spruce and beech. At one point I noticed a beech with many small perforations in its trunk about six feet from the ground and I asked Greenie if he could explain those strange incisions. "They were made by a yellow-bellied sapsucker, a member of the woodpecker tribe," he said. "From those punctures the sap of the tree exudes. It's sweet, and attracts many aphids and flies. The sapsucker then comes back and collects quite a bounty."

A bog, presumably the work of beavers whose dam has blocked drainage and caused flooding, expands a clearing in the forest as the trapped water kills young spruces and grasses by depriving their roots of oxygen. Eventually, dead vegetation will fill the bog and cause it to dry up enough for land plants to spring up again—and a new generation of spruces will reassert the forest's claim to the land.

We soon emerged from the woods into a beaver swamp, perhaps half a mile long, ankle deep in mud and drowned moss. It was now 2:45 in the afternoon. The sky was overcast, the air hot and muggy. In the distance we could see the slopes of Mount Ampersand through the haze.

The swamp was alive with birds, as Greenie had predicted. From the surrounding black spruce we could hear the call of the olive-sided fly-catcher, which has been translated by ornithologists into something that sounds like "Hic! Three beers." And from unseen sanctuaries we heard the notes of the black and white warbler and the Blackburnian warbler. On a spruce branch high above we espied the profile of a great-crested flycatcher and wished he would descend upon some of the flies that were now clustering around our heads.

Despite the threat of an approaching thunderstorm, Greenie lingered here, calling my attention to the fact that the area we stood in, uncomfortably, was a typical northern swamp, only enhanced by the beaver. The depression had been carved by glaciers during the last ice age, filled with meltwater when the glaciers receded, then deteriorated from a lake to a pond to a bog, and perhaps half a century ago became the site of a beaver dam. I was glad when we climbed out of the swamp and emerged on a ridge leading to higher ground.

"I guess we've lost our bear," Greenie said.

"That's okay with me," I said.

We now were headed back on an easterly course toward the highway, over a duff trail through balsam and spruce, white birch and pine, yellow birch and hemlock. At one point we passed on our right a pond that was pure emerald green and looked solid enough to walk upon. "That's called a seep spring," Greenie explained. "And what you see is simply sphagnum moss carpeted over water collected in a sag." Now the forest became mixed again, with huge maples and yellow birch and black cherry mingling with the conifers. Thunder rumbled in the distance. "Like me," said Greenie, "it's groaning from the heat."

We walked along through the woods for a while in silence and then, shortly before we again heard the sounds of traffic on Highway 3, we came to a cluster of huge boulders upholstered with moss and lichens.

"I don't know why the glacier decided to unload its cargo here," Greenie said. "But that's one reason I like to walk in the woods. The forest is full of surprises."

As we emerged from the woods onto the highway, about a mile away from where we had parked the car, a broad-winged hawk soared overhead, circled, and uttered one petulant cry.

We had seen no deer despite all the pellets on the runway. So I paid a visit a few days later to an old friend of mine, Koert Du Bois Burnham, whose father, John Bird Burnham, an explorer and naturalist, had acquired land between Keeseville and Willsboro, a vast tract including several lakes and mountains. During his lifetime John Burnham's estate, Highlands, was a rendezvous for such dedicated outdoorsmen as President Theodore Roosevelt; Dan Beard, a founder of the Boy Scouts of America; and the artist-naturalist Ernest Thompson Seton. The present estate includes a deer park enclosed by a wire fence, with a feeding station situated only a few yards away from the picture window at the western end of the main house. Koert and his wife, Florence, attract the animals with such delicacies as fruits and vegetables. The deer usually appear at the cocktail hour.

That was why I went up to Highlands; I hoped I could have a conversation with a deer. "No problem," Koert said, offering me a drink. And, sure enough, a few minutes later a young buck appeared out of the woods and made for the feeding station, inspecting the fare with an epicurean eye. I asked Koert if the deer would snub me and retreat if I approached, and what he would suggest as a good tactical maneuver.

"I'll give you a piece of angel food cake," he said. "Walk out slowly with the cake in your hand and say, 'Here, Dicky. Here, Dicky, Dicky, Dicky.' Then give him the cake."

So I took the cake, walked out to the wire fence, held the cake out in front of me so it would be clearly visible, and said, "Hello, Dicky. Here, Dicky, Dicky, Dicky."

The deer looked at me suspiciously, warily, but waited until I faced him squarely through the fence. I then presented the cake. Dicky looked at it with what I could interpret only as indifference, or perhaps scorn, and then turned his back and with a haughty twitch of his white tail vanished into the woods.

I returned to the house and told Koert what had happened. What had I done wrong? Why did I get such a brush-off?

"Oh, gosh," he said. "It was my fault. I gave you a piece of plain cake. He'll eat angel food cake only if it has a chocolate icing."

Prelude to Winter

PHOTOGRAPHS BY GEORGE TICE

As the early November winds rip the last leaves from the trees, the Adirondack wilderness enters a somber but beautiful demiseason that links the bright exuberance of fall with the silent snowbound winter. Long vistas open up in the woods, so that during rare bursts of sun the eye is drawn to the glitter of distant frost-coated peaks. But usually at this time of year dull gray clouds hang over the wilderness, the monochromatic light turning the mountains into a backdrop of cardboard cutouts. Often, too, the Adirondack air is veiled by a thin mist that makes wavering shadows of solid tree trunks and transforms the great boulders scattered throughout the woods into brooding giants.

It is a time of sharply isolated sounds: the honk of Canada geese flying southward in their arrow formations; the flap of dead paper-birch bark, peeling off to reveal a new pink growth; the startling crunch of the lightest of footsteps on frost-matted leaves. And almost always the wind moans its accompaniment through stiff birch, beech and maple branches, bottle-green pine and spruce, and feathery hemlock.

The busy, sparkling lakes of summer are changing now to frigid mirrors of the bared branches and leaden skies. Frogs and turtles are burrowing deep into the mud for their winter sleep. One by one the waterfowl—teal, wood ducks, mallards and black ducks—desert their summer home, among the last to leave being the hooded mergansers and the loons, whose haunting cry symbolizes summer on these Adirondack waters. Throughout the surrounding forests, animals (pages 122-123) are taking their last chance to stock up for the winter on the fall harvest of nuts, berries and fruits before the coming of the snow.

Yet to a trained eye, this time is more than the shutdown of a fruitful year or the pause before winter. Throughout the brooding forests are myriad half-hidden signs of spring. In the place of virtually every fallen leaf is a bud containing a tiny embryo leaf wrapped in tough protective scales—each a blueprint for the explosive growth to come. Brown cones dot the edges of the tamarack's bare branches and bob atop the white pine, ready for hungry birds to attack them and scatter their seeds. These—and other—clues to seasons coming, and seasons past, make November a time of special richness in the Adirondacks.

A pale November moon shines hazily through a stand of tall paper birch, throwing the bare branches into relief and reflecting off the smooth bark.

In the High Peaks area, rays of morning
sunlight, filtering through paper
and yellow birches, have strength to
melt—but not enough to evaporate—
the frost on a leaf-littered boulder.

This alder was slashed by a rutting buck to mark his territory during the mating season.

Storing Up for a Winter Siege

Throughout the Adirondacks each animal prepares for the lean months ahead in its own particular way. The mating instinct of the white-tailed deer, aroused now to ensure that the young will be born in the warm spring, is at its height, and in the many forest enclaves the smell of musk hangs in the air. After mating, the deer stay active throughout the winter, browsing on twigs, as does the snowshoe hare—which, like the short-tailed weasel, changes to a winter white *(page 122).*

Other animals are preparing to spend most of their winter asleep, stuffing themselves with food to build up warm, nourishing layers of fat or, as some insects do, pupating or laying eggs to survive the cold.

The bear sleeps deeply but comes out occasionally to snuffle about, then dozes off again. The more active beaver leaves its lodge by an underwater exit to nibble at a kitchen garden of tender twigs it has stored in the mud under the ice.

A very few creatures, such as the woodchuck, chipmunk, jumping mouse and some bats, curl up in true hibernation, their metabolism undergoing radical changes. The body temperature of the woodchuck drops from 100° to between 57° and 40°, while its respiration rate slows from about 35 to five breaths a minute. And from December through March these hibernators may stir only to stretch, take a deep breath and then resume their sleep till spring.

Tightly packed beech branches, stripped of their nuts, are leftovers from the fall feast of tree-climbing black bears.

A snowshoe hare licks clean the patches of thick white winter fur that have begun to replace his summer coat of reddish brown. This winter growth, besides providing warmth and camouflage, gives extra surface area to the hare's feet, making it easier for the animal to bound over deep snow.

A muskrat emerges through thin ice, dragging vegetation from the stream. Muskrats do not store food for the whole winter in their burrows; they go out regularly to forage, leaving and entering by underwater portals. When swimming in frozen waterways they breathe air trapped under the ice.

An early snow lies lightly on the tumbled rocks of an Adirondack brook. Though the water still bubbles along its bed and through gaps and crevices, collars of ice are already spreading inward from the shallow edges of the stream where the water runs slow, and outward from the cold stones in its center. Soon the stream, throttled by ice, will disappear completely under a thickening mantle of snow.

5/ The Bounteous Waters

Bless the face of running water!

ROBERT LOUIS STEVENSON/ *LETTER FROM SARANAC LAKE,* 1887

I was somewhat appalled when George Davis, Assistant Director of the Adirondack Park Agency, told me our rendezvous next morning would be at 7 a.m. Since my house on Lake Champlain is an hour's drive from the agency's headquarters at Ray Brook, outside the village of Saranac Lake, I would have to wrench myself from bed around 5 a.m., an hour at which I am seldom perpendicular.

"Well, you wanted a white-water canoe trip," George said, sensing a slight tension over the phone, "and the Moose River is on the western edge of the park, just inside the Blue Line. It takes three hours to drive all the way across the park, so if we leave from Ray Brook here at seven, we can be in the canoes a little after ten—allowing for a bite of breakfast at Old Forge."

It was true that I had suggested a canoe trip in the western reaches of the Adirondacks. I had spent most of my life in the northeast quadrant, which encompasses Lake Champlain and the High Peaks, with occasional sorties to the central enclaves around Lake Placid, the Saranac Lakes, Tupper Lake, and perhaps twice to Fourth Lake in the Fulton Chain. But the far western fringe of the park, where the woods begin to thin and the land starts to slope down to the Black River plain, was unexplored territory for me.

George had chosen the Moose River for our trip for several reasons. "To begin with, I think it's one of the finest rivers in the Adirondacks," he had said a few days earlier, "second perhaps only to the Hudson. A lot of people would argue for the special beauties of the Ausable, the Saranac and the Raquette, but the Moose in my opinion is actually one of the three or four great rivers of the Adirondacks. It rises in the heart of the area, and its three branches run through all kinds of Adirondack terrain before they meet below Old Forge. There is not much about the Moose River in Adirondack literature; and it's not much used today, which is another reason I picked it out for our trip. Besides," he added, "it has one of the finest white-water stretches in the entire Adirondacks. We're going to run that."

So, the following morning, the first day of July, I found myself on the road to Ray Brook, filled with a mixture of anticipation and anxiety. Over the years my own pleasure has focused on climbing. But of the nine million persons who invade the Adirondacks each year, I am in an insignificant minority. The overwhelming majority (excluding the winter skiers) come to enjoy the profusion of lakes and rivers that spangle and striate the region. Few, if any, parks in the country have so much water. Within the Adirondack Park there are more than 6,000 miles of rivers and streams. In addition, the park is bejeweled with some 2,000 lakes, of which at least 50 measure more than a square mile in size. No hiker or camper needs to carry a canteen, save perhaps above timberline. Elsewhere all the visitor requires is a cup, or even the cupped palm of his hand.

Before the dissection of the Adirondack country by roads and railroads in the 19th Century, the interweaving of these lakes and rivers provided a network of transportation for both Indians and early settlers. Later the Hudson, the Oswegatchie, the Saint Regis and Schroon rivers all served as routes for lumbermen. Today the Raquette River, flowing out of Raquette Lake through Long Lake to Tupper Lake, provides canoeists with an uninterrupted trip of more than 50 miles. And our own chosen river, the Moose, intersects and connects with almost a hundred lakes, ponds and tributary streams.

There is a rich variety to the Adirondack lakes. Some have rocky shores, some white sandy beaches. Some are surrounded by swamps and mud. Except for those that are undergoing eutrophication, either from natural causes or through human abuse, most have clear, spring-fed water—cool in summer, ice-armored in winter sometimes to a thickness of three feet.

Every Adirondack resident or visitor has his favorite among these lakes, the gem he thinks reflects the purest ray serene. Blue Mountain

Lake, by virtue of its forested shores, sapphire waters and the symmetrical peak rising like a sculptured monument at its northern end, has been the most popularly acclaimed. Lake George won the affection of Thomas Jefferson, who, while serving as Secretary of State before becoming President, visited its shores with James Madison in 1791, and paid it a memorable tribute in a letter to his daughter, written, in the fashion of many a later Adirondack letter, on birch bark. "Lake George is without comparison the most beautiful water I ever saw," Jefferson wrote, "formed by a contour of mountains into a basin 35 miles long, and from 2 to 4 miles broad, finely interspersed with islands, its waters limpid as chrystal & the mountain sides covered with rich groves of . . . silver fir, white pine, Aspen and paper birch down to the water edge, here and there precipices of rock to chequer the scene & save it from monotony. An abundance of speckled trout, salmon trout, bass and other fish with which it is stored, have added to our other amusements, the sport of taking them."

But my personal favorite—apart from Lake Champlain—is Elk Lake, nestled at the foot of the Dix range, completely girdled by mountains, studded with evergreen islets, and comparatively little known since it lies deep within privately owned forest land. Today, still secluded, Elk Lake is open to hikers and canoeists, but it is strictly off limits to motorboats and hunters.

The sun had already leaped the rampart of Vermont's Green Mountains when I climbed into my car and headed west from Lake Champlain toward Ray Brook. No clouds marbled the pale blue sky, but as I approached the village of Elizabethtown, I noted that the eastern High Peaks were blurred by midsummer haze—a welcome sign of a warm day to come. The main street was devoid of cars and pedestrians when I passed the red-and-white county courthouse where John Brown's portrait hangs above the judge's bench. His body had lain there on the night of December 6-7, 1859, en route to his home in North Elba following his raid on Harpers Ferry and subsequent execution in Charles Town, Virginia.

I reflected as I drove on that few people among the millions who have sung "John Brown's body lies a-mouldering in the grave" know that his grave, marked by a plaque attached to a huge glacial boulder and surrounded by an iron fence, is situated on a windy eminence just three miles southeast of Lake Placid. The farmhouse where he had given sanctuary to fugitive slaves and tried unsuccessfully to establish a self-sufficient Negro colony still stands, furnished as he last saw it.

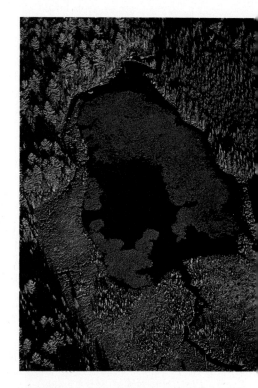

Two dramatic signs of natural eutrophication (the process of a pond's gradual shrinkage and death) are visible in this aerial view of Hyslop Pond, near Vanderwhacker Mountain. The smartweed and water lilies now covering most of the pond's surface will spread; as the plants die off seasonally they will sink and accumulate in layers, making the pond ever shallower by raising the level of the bottom. Meanwhile, a small inlet builds a new, encroaching shoreline.

He was laid to rest on a cold, rainy day, December 8, 1859, following a ceremony conducted by a minister from Vermont, who was ostracized by his congregation on his return to his church.

The road out of Elizabethtown climbs steadily to the crest of Spruce Hill, drops down into Keene Valley, and curves westward past the Elm Tree Inn at Keene, dominated by what is probably the oldest and largest American elm in the Adirondacks (80 feet tall and five feet in diameter at its base). The route then climbs again past the narrow Cascade Lakes—two of the darkest and most dramatic glacial lakes in the Adirondacks, sunlit only at high noon. It then emerges onto the high plains of North Elba, swings by the Olympic bobsled run at Mount Van Hoevenberg, and then past John Brown's farm until it connects with what is known as the Old Military Road, which leads to Ray Brook. I arrived there a few minutes after 7 a.m. to be greeted by my friend Clarence Petty, airplane pilot and Forest Preserve Specialist for the Adirondack Park Agency.

"George and Anita have taken off with the canoes," Clarence said. "We'll meet them at Old Forge." Anita Riner is a specialist on the staff of the agency, with the title of Natural Resource Planner. I parked my car and transferred my small parachute-silk knapsack, containing a sandwich, a couple of cans of beer and a first-aid kit, to Clarence's official agency sedan. As we pointed west through the town of Saranac Lake, I remembered that Saranac Lake was once the nation's most famous center for research and therapy in tuberculosis, a disease for which the only medication had once been a bottle of cough mixture —and for which positive diagnosis amounted to a sentence of death.

In the summer of 1873 a dashing young doctor named Edward Livingston Trudeau, a TB victim, came to Saranac Lake to die. He spent two summers there and, having survived, decided to stay on through the winter—which few tuberculosis victims then dared to do. It was a historic decision, for Trudeau lived on at Saranac Lake for 41 years, and not only resumed the practice of medicine but also became internationally renowned as a pioneer in tuberculosis care and founder of the world-famous Trudeau Sanatorium. Trudeau's anti-TB treatment methods were based on the therapeutically clean air of the Adirondack wilderness. His patients, even the bedridden ones, spent all their time outdoors. Summer and winter they passed their days taking mild exercise or resting on a roofed but open porch, wrapped in cold weather in a cocoon of blankets, breathing the clear mountain air. More often than not, as in the case of Trudeau himself, the disease was arrested if not cured. After World War II, when new techniques of combating the TB bacillus were developed, many of the laboratories that had grown up around Saranac Lake in the wake of the Trudeau clinic turned to other medical projects. But the pioneer has not been forgotten. A life-sized bronze statue of Trudeau by the sculptor Gutzon Borglum overlooks the Trudeau Institute on Lower Saranac Lake.

Continuing westward, we skirted the south shore of Upper Saranac Lake, and my thoughts again ranged backward, this time to the many great men who had been drawn for one reason or another to these broad uplands. Robert Louis Stevenson, himself a victim of tuberculosis, spent the winter of 1887-1888 at Saranac Lake, where he not only enjoyed a remission of his illness but also turned out 12 essays for *Scribner's Magazine,* and a novel, *The Master of Ballantrae.* Mark Twain maintained a summer camp on Lower Saranac Lake for many years. And in 1858 on the shore of Follensby Pond southwest of the Saranacs, a glittering group of Boston literati established a so-called Philosophers' Camp, whose membership reads like an honor list of 19th Century American scholars. Included were Ralph Waldo Emerson; James Russell Lowell; Professor Louis Agassiz, the distinguished zoologist-geologist; John Holmes, the brother of Oliver Wendell Holmes; and assorted friends. At the outset they had urged Henry Wadsworth Longfellow to join them. "Is it true that Emerson is going to take a gun?" he asked. When the reply was affirmative, Longfellow exclaimed: "Then someone will be shot!" and refused the invitation.

As we drove farther along toward Tupper Lake, Clarence said to me, "I hope you're looking forward to this white-water canoeing. You know it's not the safest sport in the world. You can get sideswiped by the current, capsize, get hung up on a boulder, and even drown. People usually don't understand the real power of the water that propels them: it amounts to hundreds of tons per second. I've seen an aluminum canoe bent like a hairpin around a boulder—and if you get caught between the canoe and a rock, there's no way out."

"It sounds very much to me," I observed, "as though your chosen element is air rather than water."

"Right," said Clarence. "I'd much rather be flying an airplane today."

After passing through the lumber town of Tupper Lake, we turned southeast toward Long Lake on a two-lane highway that, like so many other roads in the center of the park, runs mile after mile through a green, leafy corridor. The area is agleam with pure lakes and ponds and rivers and streams, all excellent trout water. Inevitably known as the Lake Country, it harbors many so-called Adirondack camps—a singularly undescriptive word for the rustic estates established there not long after the Civil War.

In the late 1860s and 1870s, wealthy residents of New York City became aware of the wilderness not too many miles from their Fifth Avenue and Riverside Drive mansions. With a rush, the Morgans, Lehmans, Rockefellers, Vanderbilts, Whitneys and others began acquiring enormous tracts of lakeshore property, with thousands of surrounding acres of forest to buffer them against the outside world. At the edges of their lakes, they erected their camps.

The grand prototype of the Adirondack camp was conceived and built by William West Durant, son of Union Pacific founder Thomas Durant. The younger Durant's home combined the woodsy features of a log cabin with the decorative frills of a Swiss chalet adorned with gables, balconies and ornamental wood carving. When Durant felt a need to expand, he built detached guesthouses, servants' quarters, storage facilities and a boathouse that included both a music room and dance floor on a mezzanine above the boats. These he connected by covered runways to the central lodge, with its high, crossbeamed rooms and enormous fireplaces. In the Lake Country I have seen many such camps, where it is possible to walk perhaps a quarter of a mile through a labyrinth of roofed-over boardwalks, protected from rain or snow for the entire distance.

As decades passed, variant tastes produced other eccentricities—on Upper Saint Regis Lake one man, impressed by a trip to the Far East, imported Japanese artisans to remodel his camp in authentic Japanese style, and even put all his maids into kimonos. Another re-created on the shore of Schroon Lake a baronial German castle, and stocked the surrounding woods with wild boars. Another constructed a 17th Century French château, complete with crenelated battlements and towers, and girdled by a network of formal gardens. The camp was set in the midst of an estate of 8,654 acres, enclosed by an eight-foot-high fence. The château was constructed of Adirondack stone, shaped and fitted by some 50 masons imported from Italy. In places, some of the outer walls are six feet thick.

The sun was rising higher as Clarence and I continued along toward the pyramid of Blue Mountain. Rounding it, we came upon the lake it guards. Between 1880 and 1900, Blue Mountain Lake was *the* place in

Framed by red and orange maple leaves, evergreens and greenish yellow birch foliage, a small cove at the southwestern end of Elk Lake glows on an early October afternoon.

the Adirondacks, regarded by some as healthier than a European spa, and a rival to Newport and Bar Harbor for the carriage trade. Today, beautiful as ever, the lake boasts an even greater distinction, for it is the home of the splendid Adirondack Museum, whose galleries and exhibition halls house a priceless collection of paintings, books, photographs, and artifacts ranging from Indian relics to Adirondack guide boats, private railroad cars and carriages—all shown in a complex of handsome buildings interspersed with lawns and gardens on the slope of Blue Mountain, overlooking the lake.

Farther along, between Raquette Lake and Old Forge, where we were to join George and Anita, the road twisted through the Fulton Chain Lakes, named for Robert Fulton. In 1811, just four years after his historic voyage up the Hudson in the steamboat *Clermont,* Fulton was asked by the New York State Legislature to serve on a commission created to explore the possibility of a trans-Adirondack water route between the Hudson River and the Great Lakes. He submitted an enthusiastic report on the Chain. But a less demanding canal along the Mohawk toward Erie was being surveyed at the same time—and the Erie Canal won out: it was opened for navigation in 1825.

A few minutes after 10 a.m., with the July sun now hot and high, we arrived at Old Forge. We noted that George and Anita had preceded us. Their four-wheel-drive vehicle, with two aluminum canoes lashed to its top, stood outside a coffee shop. When Clarence and I walked in, George and Anita hailed us. Anita is a slender, attractive girl with brown hair and eyes, and a bright smile. If she was going to run the rapids, why was I worrying?

"Well," said George, "I suppose on the drive over, Clarence fed you a line on the perils of white-water canoeing. I hope you didn't take it seriously. He feels safe only in an airplane."

Clarence smiled faintly but said nothing.

"Shall we get going?" George suggested. "I've got life jackets for all of us. You know it's foolish to do white-water canoeing without them. They're very compact, made of foam, not at all like the old Mae West types of World War II vintage."

George paid his check and, as he waited for his change, added that the Moose River was low, below normal for this time of year.

"Is that good news or bad news?" I asked.

"Both," he said. "It's good news because the volume of water will be less than it is during the spring runoff. It's bad news because when the water is low you're more likely to get hung up on rocks. The normal

flow rate of the Moose, computed on an annual scale, is 807 cubic feet
per second. But as with all rivers the flow rate varies. The maximum recorded figure is 18,700 cubic feet per second. The minimum recorded
rate is 42 cubic feet per second. So, as I say, we're a little bit below the
norm today. So keep your eyes peeled."

About ten miles southwest of Old Forge we crossed the Moose at the
hamlet of McKeever and unloaded the canoes at the top of an embankment perhaps 15 feet above a stretch of still water. We then drove
on—George and Anita in the four-wheel-drive vehicle, Clarence and I
in the sedan—and pulled into an old logging road thrusting into the
woods about eight miles west of McKeever. It was a terrible road, rut-
ty, overgrown with brush, but we managed to get down to the riverbank.
There we left the four-wheel-drive to pick up the canoes at the end of
our trip down the river. The four of us then piled into the sedan and
headed back to McKeever, put on our life jackets and in a moment
were afloat on tranquil, unruffled brown water. George and Anita led
the way. Clarence and I followed. I asked Clarence why the water was
so brown. Was it polluted?

"No," he said. "Dark water is typical of a lot of Adirondack streams.
The pigments come from organic acids produced by the decomposition
of leaves and bark that fall into the river. As you can see, the banks
here are dense with vegetation. Also, many of the boulders in the stream
contain iron, which is leached out by the flow of water."

I looked away from the water, up the wooded banks, and saw a
mixed forest of red maple, yellow birch, red spruce, black cherry and
hemlock cresting the rim of the river. On the lower embankment, flowering azaleas flashed their ruby lights amid raspberry bushes, thorn apples and other woody shrubs.

A faint breeze from the west produced ripples on the water and kept
the Adirondack blackflies ashore. The image of white water seemed far
away. This tranquil stream, perhaps a hundred feet wide, could not possibly be a threat. It barely moved as we paddled slowly downstream, I
in the bow, Clarence in the stern. From time to time we could hear the
ethereal notes of a white-throated sparrow. And now, abruptly, a trout
broke the surface of the water in pursuit of a fly.

"That was a brown trout," Clarence pointed out. "Upstream you'll
find other members of the family—brook trout, rainbow trout—they
like the cooler waters. But on the lower stretches of rivers, the water is
warmer and only the brown trout seem to enjoy it."

At this moment, George called back from his canoe, which floated perhaps 75 feet ahead of ours. "Can you hear the first rapids?"

Faintly I became aware of a deep crescendo of sound. It sent a few tremors up my spine, but the tempo of the river remained slow. I glanced up at a great red maple and saw, on an overhanging branch, the perky crest of a kingfisher searching for fish below. When I looked ahead again from my seat in the bow, I saw something white. It was not peaceful white, like bed linen or snow. It was more like the movement of clouds in a squall. Meanwhile the bass voice of the river grew louder, and our forward movement quickened.

"Here we go," George called back. He was kneeling in the bow to reconnoiter the best route through the rocks and riffs, shouting orders to Anita in the stern. Clarence and I back-paddled, holding our position in the accelerating current until we saw that they had successfully negotiated the rapids and were drifting in the still water below.

"Okay," Clarence said, "we'll follow their course." A few strokes of our paddles brought us into the swift current. We began to move—fast. Clarence, in the stern, was steersman. Kneeling in the bow, I had two functions: to try to spot submerged boulders ahead and indicate by pointing whether to veer port or starboard; and to use my paddle to deflect us from a collision course.

We ran the rapids without incident, and joined George and Anita below the rift.

"How'd you like it?" George asked, grinning.

"It brought back memories," I said, "of roller coasters and chute-the-chutes at Coney Island. It was fun."

With little effort we paddled through quieter water, between the forest walls and their riparian foundations of great flat rocks overhung with hemlock boughs. At one point we passed a huge dead pine; on one projecting branch perched a great horned owl, alone and aloof. It clung there as though frozen, without moving its head. Then we again heard rapids roar ahead and, minutes thereafter, as we rounded a promontory, saw stilettos of furious water stabbing the air.

"This one will be tougher," George shouted. "Be careful."

Here, the river was about 120 feet wide and we could make out several possible channels. George chose to run like a fullback straight down the middle, and we followed his route, between rocks that towered ominously on either side above a rushing frenzy of foam. Then we reached another patch of still water; and I thought as I looked down on the placid surface aglitter with the noonday sun, that with rivers, as with

A female rainbow trout, heading upstream to lay her eggs, executes an acrobatic leap on the Bouquet River. Native to the West Coast, rainbows were imported into the Adirondacks a century ago as game fish prized for endurance and fighting qualities.

women, quiet is vastly more delightful than turbulence. As this extraordinary insight occurred to me, a family of wood ducks, mother and four ducklings, paddled serenely in a line across our bows, apparently headed for a picnic lunch on the left bank.

Again, the roar sounded ahead, and this time George signaled us to follow him into a small cove in the lee of a gigantic boulder.

"This next one is really tough," he said, "and we may want to portage around it. It's actually kind of a waterfall with sheer walls of six or seven feet on either side of one central rift. The rift is about five feet wide, between big rocks, and the water goes very fast. There's a lot of agitation at the bottom. Stay here and let me have a quick look at it."

Clarence and I held the canoes together and chatted with Anita while George walked down the bank to inspect the rapids. He returned five minutes later and said, "It doesn't look too bad. I think we can make it. I tell you what. Anita and I'll go first. You guys lag behind and watch how we make out. Then if it looks okay, follow us—or if it looks too rough, carry around it."

We pushed off, and as we neared the rapids the voice of the Moose sounded in my ears like thunder. Clarence and I maintained our position at the brink, and watched George and Anita disappear in a blizzard of water, then emerge, their canoe bucking wildly, at the bottom of the chute. Clarence asked me if I wanted to run it or make the carry around the rapids. I said: "What the hell, let's try it." He said: "Okay, it's your decision."

Three or four strokes of our paddles and we were headed for the rift, past the point of no return. Kneeling in the bow, I saw we had no options. The current caught us, hurled us into the rift and swept us down between the rocks toward the foam below. Then suddenly—CRUNCH! Clarence and I pitched forward, our motion halted, while the river raced past and began to swing our canoe broadside to the current. We had foundered on an underwater boulder, invisible to me amid the froth, and now we were hung up, inexorably pivoting.

"Careful now," Clarence shouted. "Take your paddle and push lightly against the rock at your left. I'll see what I can do back here, and maybe we can straighten out."

I followed instructions, poking gently, and we moved a few inches. But we continued to swing broadside to the current. Then without warning, we capsized, and I found myself in a tumult of blind racing water, hurled about by forces I could not oppose. I have always been a pretty

good swimmer, and my life jacket now helped me rise to the surface
—but when I emerged, I could see nothing, for I had come up beneath
the overturned canoe, which was wedged between the rocks on either
side of the rift.

I fought my way out, saw the blessed light of day and was swept immediately downstream. Although the right bank lay scarcely 50 feet
away, it was unreachable. I caught a glimpse of Clarence, swimming toward the left bank, trying to haul our canoe behind him. Somehow I
had clung to my paddle, because George had told us when we started
that no extra paddles could be had—"So hang on to them." Stroking
with my right arm, I managed to navigate a diagonal course to shore,
landing a hundred yards downstream from the rift.

When I emerged at last onto a flat, shelving boulder, I realized my
knees were bruised from ricochets off the rocks. My right index finger
was covered with blood from a gash I must have gotten from some
rough edge on the canoe. George came hastening up the left bank, leaving Anita in a cove, and helped Clarence free our canoe from its rocky
berth. George tore up a handkerchief and bandaged my finger. In our accident Clarence and I had lost not only our sandwiches and beer, but
our first-aid kit as well.

Studying his map, George announced that we were just about halfway between our two cars, and there was no choice but to continue
moving downstream. He added that ahead of us lay two rapids even
more dangerous than the last one; we would have no option but to
carry around both of them.

Afloat again, I asked Clarence what tactical or navigational sins we
had committed. "None," he said. "You and I together outweigh George
and Anita by at least a hundred pounds. So they skimmed through that
rift without any trouble. We just rode lower in the water. We didn't do
anything wrong at all."

As the afternoon wore on, we moved down the Moose River, through
still waters and unmenacing riffles, portaging around the savage rapids,
to the Blue Line at the western frontier of the Adirondack Park. The carries were painful—my knees hurt and my finger bled, and at every portage we had to scramble up a steep bank, thick with bracken, raspberry
and blueberry bushes, alders, mountain-holly, thorn apples and wild-
raisin. After surmounting the bank each time we had to bushwhack
through woods choked with undergrowth, carrying our canoes, ha-
rassed constantly by Adirondack blackflies and deerflies. At one point,

when we paused to rest, a deerfly lighted on my hand. Before I could take defensive action it excised a small morsel of my flesh and flew away to savor it in solitude.

At the last portage, I stood on a rock ledge and looked down at a maelstrom from which I think no one could have escaped. The geological formation was comparable to the one that had dunked Clarence and me —but more extreme and fearsome. Rock cliffs descended vertically from either side of a central rift, through which an incalculable tonnage of water hurtled down to what could only be described as a hole in the river. Over and above the major current, water flooded in from either side and submerged boulders directly below formed a kind of dike that sent the water crashing back again into the hole, violent and turbulent as ocean surf.

About 5 p.m. we carried our canoes ashore for the last time. The sun still rode high, and the air was hot, heavy and humid. The flies clustered around us. With relief we got into our respective cars. Clarence and I drove northeastward in relative silence. "Well, I'm sorry about our accident," he said after a while.

"That's okay," I said. "At least we did it."

After a three-hour drive through the gradually darkening forests of the western and central Adirondacks, lighted intermittently by the neon signs of scattered hamlets and towns, we reached Ray Brook, where we parted company. I climbed into my own car and headed home. It was dark when I arrived and the surface of Champlain was unruffled —tranquil waters, good waters to sleep beside.

An Obdurate Mountain Passage

PHOTOGRAPHS BY JOHN DOMINIS

Avalanche Pass, a rugged four-mile cleft in the mountains between Marcy Dam and the southern end of Lake Colden, owes its name to the dramatic impression the place made on the first white men who saw it in 1836. These explorers were iron prospectors with names like David Henderson, Archibald McIntyre and David C. Colden, which they freely conferred on neighboring mountains and other natural features; but these hard-bitten egoists were so struck by immense, chaotic falls of rock—the result of weathering and erosion from the mountainsides—as to forget themselves and simply christen the place Avalanche.

Over the years, much of this loose rock has been mantled by soil and vegetation, although many a monument such as the one at right emerges to remind the traveler of the prospectors' inspiration. Actually it was not only the rockfalls but also glaciation that shaped the landscape. Before the last ice ages, the narrow valley between Avalanche Mountain and Mount Colden carried a small stream. When the glaciers retreated about 10,000 years ago, they had deepened the valley and deposited rocky debris that blocked the stream to form Avalanche Lake and Lake Colden. (A third lake, Flowed Land, created when the outlet of Lake Colden was dammed in the late 1800s, lies just south of the pass.)

Today, as a result of its harsh evolution, Avalanche Pass is an obdurate place. For most of its length, the going is steep, strenuous and moist. Cliffs rise vertically on both sides, cutting off sunlight except for a few hours around noon. At Avalanche Lake, the path vanishes and is replaced by a system of log bridges that often disappear under knee-deep water as a result of busy dam-building by beavers.

In the dimness and damp inside the pass, the mood is oppressive, dominated by the narrowness of the trail and the high, steep walls. One way to change moods and regain a sense of the area's majesty is to ascend Mount Colden, climbing a precipitous natural staircase called the Trap Dike; the route was actually carved by erosion, which wore away a vein of softer rock in the tough Precambrian anorthosite to form a trough. From the top of Colden, the region of Avalanche Pass can be seen as a breathtaking panorama set against the background of the virtually trackless mountains that stretch to the southwest.

Its outlines softened by moss and lichen, a monolithic remnant of a post-ice-age rockfall dwarfs the trunks of century-old fir trees beside the trail at the bottom of Avalanche Pass.

Dappled with light at midday—the only time when full sunlight penetrates the depths of the pass—poplars and birches mask the sheer walls bordering the trail near Avalanche Lake.

The bare, eroded face of Mount Colden, seen here from the opposite side of the pass on Avalanche Mountain, supports only a few birches. In the foreground is the Trap Dike, a deep cleft running steeply up the side of the mountain like a giant stepladder.

Seen from a different vantage point on Avalanche Mountain, the Trap Dike —the most direct route up Mount Colden from Avalanche Pass—reveals its sheer-sided depths. The vein of coarse igneous rock that once filled the chasm has long since eroded away.

The U shape of the valley, seen clearly at Avalanche Lake, is the result of glaciation. The cliffs in the foreground owe their steepness to massive erosive forces that deposited debris at the bottom of the pass, which is now concealed under the lake's waters.

Runoff from a recent rain cascades
down an escarpment on the Avalanche
Pass side of Mount Colden. Destined
to contribute to the vast waterway of
the Hudson, such ephemeral falls are
an integral part of the erosion process.

Close to timberline, frost action has
cracked the stone face of Mount Colden
and has piled rock slabs into jagged
overhangs. The last few hundred feet
of trail to the top of the mountain
are reached through this narrow gap.

Viewed from the summit of Mount Colden, Avalanche Pass dissolves into the southwestern wilds of the High Peaks region. Beyond Lake

Colden (foreground) the eye is drawn past Flowed Land to Lake Henderson in the distance and the Santanoni Mountains on the horizon.

6/ The Great Pass

A slightly flawed paradise is…the best we deserve; certainly the best we have been able to keep.

PAUL JAMIESON/ *PREFACE, AN ADIRONDACK READER*

Within their bright tapestry of mountains, lakes and forests, the Adirondacks present fundamental paradoxes. These relate directly to the fact that the region is both a wilderness and a locus of human habitation and economic enterprise. Adirondack Park, largest of all parks in the United States, was created by the New York State Legislature as a natural heritage, with more than a third to be kept "forever wild" —though also, by implication, to be enjoyed. The rest remained in the hands of private owners, to be developed under certain state guidelines. As a result, the region today is a mixture of wilderness and civilization: hamlets and towns dot the forests; clusters of cottages rim the shorelines of lakes. The park is invaded in summer by campers and hikers, in winter by skiers; in a few widely scattered areas it is deeply and permanently scarred by open-pit and other mining operations. Almost everywhere there are reminders that man uses the wild Adirondacks, and that he has been doing so for a very long time.

I have known this ever since I was a boy. But I had never organized my thinking about the paradox of wilderness and human presence. As Verplanck Colvin, first great surveyor of the region, once wrote, "Few fully understand what the Adirondack wilderness really is"—and I was no exception. And so, by way of setting my thoughts in order, I decided to venture through an Adirondack enclave whose heart has remained as wild as any piece of Northeastern America: the Great Adirondack

Pass—or Indian Pass as it is now more commonly called. Here, I hoped, I would be able to find that delicate and haunting mood of preserved past, of deep forest and free winds, that is for me the essence of wilderness. But I was also well aware that, along the trail into and out of this wild place, I would find signs of man, some subtle, some disturbingly intrusive, some new and some very old. Perhaps, I thought, the very proximity of man's vestiges to the distilled wildness of the pass would finally bring the paradox into focus for me, and thus help me to penetrate the ultimate mystery articulated by Colvin.

One day in early November, therefore, when the snows had not yet trespassed below timberline, I set off with a photographer friend named Bob Walch, who had met me at my home in Westport. I had never before explored Indian Pass, but I had been fascinated by the very thought of the place ever since, as a boy, I read a description of it in Alfred L. Donaldson's classic, *A History of the Adirondacks:*

"The Indian Pass . . . is a stupendous gorge between the two mountains, Wallface and McIntyre, lying a short distance northeast of Lake Henderson. It is a mighty chasm torn apart by the convulsions of nature. About a mile in length, its sheer walls rise in places to one thousand feet and more. . . . It was once much deeper, but repeated slides of rock and earth have raised the present base and made it weirdly rough and tortuous. In consequence of this, one of the striking features of the place is the large number of huge boulders, often plumed with trees, that seem balanced in precarious poises, yet are found to be securely rooted against the powerful dislodging agents that attack them. Mount McIntyre, heavily wooded, rises on one side at an angle of forty-five degrees, while on the other, Wallface Mountain presents an almost vertical precipice of naked rock. At many places in this deep abyss the ice never melts and the rays of the sun never shine."

Legend has it that the Indians called the pass *He-no-do-aw-da*—the Path of the Thunderer—because of the eerie acoustical effects produced by the reverberation of echoes from Wallface Mountain, a sound the American novelist Gertrude Atherton, describing a thunderstorm in the pass, called "Hell moving into summer quarters." No one today knows the identity of the first white man to experience the weird grandeur of the pass, but the first white men of record were a group of mining prospectors led by David Henderson, an engineer, in 1826.

After the American Revolution many veterans who had campaigned in the Champlain Valley were drawn back by the unpeopled land and the promises it held forth—forests, farms, furs. Others had noticed orange- and russet-colored veins of iron in boulders along stream beds and on mountain slides. An early settlement at North Elba, near Lake Placid, grew up around a forge established by Henderson and his father-in-law, Archibald McIntyre, in 1809. Though quantities of ore existed in the vicinity much of it proved inferior, and the works failed in 1815. But McIntyre and Henderson persisted in their prospecting, and a decade later were rewarded by a sensational strike, proclaimed by Henderson as "the most extraordinary bed of iron ore . . . which perhaps this North American continent affords."

As Henderson described the discovery in a letter of October 14, 1826, he and some friends were setting forth to hunt for veins of ore when they were approached by "a strapping young Indian of a Canadian tribe" who had a small piece of iron ore in his blanket. He said it had come from a notch in the Great Pass, and offered to take the Henderson party there. Despite some doubts Henderson agreed, since the Indian appeared to be "a very modest, honest looking fellow" and asked only "Dollar, half, & 'bacco" for his services. Under the Indian's guidance, Henderson and his companions proceeded to the spot, a journey of four arduous days. The notch, Henderson wrote, was "as wild a place as I ever saw . . . a terrific place." He noted the existence of two streams —which still flow today from the summit of the notch—and identified the northern of the two as "the very fountain head of the Ausable River." The other trickles southward to form the Hudson. Eventually both tributaries reach the Atlantic Ocean—at points more than 750 miles apart. Yet at their source the springs are so close together that, as a 19th Century observer noted, "the wildcat lapping the water of the one may bathe his rear feet in the other."

After camping that night on the southern slope of the pass, the group continued downstream and soon began to see pieces of iron ore, "some as large as a pumpkin." Then, with mounting excitement, they found a bed of ore in the stream bed, and finally a vein on a ledge above the river, 50 feet wide. "In short, the thing was past all our conceptions. . . . Do not conceive it wonderful that this immense vein has never been discovered—it is in an extraordinary place."

To preserve the secret, Henderson and his men removed all traces of their visit, obliterating even their own footprints as they returned to North Elba to lay plans for moving and processing the ore.

Within the next decade the McIntyre Iron Works became one of the largest mining operations in the Adirondacks. A colony of some 200 engineers, workmen and their families was established around the blast furnace and the settlement soon had both a bank and a school. At various times the town was called McIntyre, Adirondac (without the k) and Tahawus (an Indian word applied to nearby Mount Marcy meaning *it cleaves the sky*).

Although the ore was abundant, it turned out to contain a mysterious impurity—later found to be titanium—and after some 20 years, the company closed down the furnace. But mining in the area resumed in 1941, with the development of titanium first as a paint pigment, then as a heat-resistant alloy ideal for use in jet engines. Near the abandoned iron works now gapes a thriving titanium mine, with a pair of 1,500-foot-long open pits.

About two miles north of the titanium mine, the vestiges of Adirondac Village have been preserved as museum pieces. Nearby is a parking lot where Bob and I, arriving in separate automobiles, left one vehicle to carry us home after our hike through the pass. We then drove back to my home at Westport to spend the night before setting off on our trip.

No snow had whitened the valleys but in November the daylight hours pass as swiftly as migrant geese, so Bob and I had to get going by dawn if we hoped to complete the traverse of the pass before dark. We parked in a large grassy area provided by the Adirondack Mountain Club. Only a few other cars stood in the lot. It was misting and we shivered inside our windbreakers as we shouldered our packs and skirted the shore of Heart Lake to the west. In the half-light we could just make out the jutting eaves of the lodge maintained for climbers by the club since 1932. The original Adirondack Lodge had been a hotel, built in 1880 by Henry van Hoevenberg. His lodge attracted considerable attention as one of the biggest log structures in the world, the exterior composed entirely of giant spruce timbers, the interior finished with fine craftsmanship and equipped with modern bathrooms. But much of the hotel's fame stemmed from the romantic tragedy that originally brought the building into existence.

Van Hoevenberg first came to the Adirondacks in 1877 with a group of friends for a camping trip on the Upper Ausable Lake. In the party was a girl named Josephine Scofield, to whom Van Hoevenberg became engaged. Later, the young lovers decided to climb Mount Marcy and from its summit select a site for their future home. They chose a tiny lake that looked to them like a heart-shaped sapphire, utterly secluded, with mountains rising sheer from its shores. They named one of the peaks Mount Jo—and so it is known today. But Jo never lived to see their home completed. She died of unknown causes within the year.

The anguished Van Hoevenberg determined to build and maintain the lodge as a memorial to his beloved. It enjoyed quiet success until it was destroyed with all the adjoining woodlands by the catastrophic forest fires of 1903. Heart Lake, Mount Jo—that small cameo of a lake and the graceful little mountain standing above it—seem a perfect memorial to a lost dream.

We rounded the curve of Heart Lake and headed along its shore toward Indian Pass, a short distance away. We quickly reached the end of the lake, about half a mile from the lodge, picking our way around puddles and muddy sags in the road that serves the scattered camps of the club complex. Then all signs of man fell behind and we began to climb to the top of a short rise.

I remarked to Bob, who had climbed extensively in the West, that he could expect quite a few steep pitches on this trip, but for every foot of altitude we gained, we would lose one soon thereafter. I explained that when we reached the height of the pass we would stand at an elevation of 2,834 feet; Heart Lake's elevation is 2,179 feet. Yet, though we would ascend a total of only 655 feet, we would climb and descend many more hundreds of feet on a roller-coaster ribbon of ups and downs. Bob grunted. He was accustomed to open trails, blue skies above, sweeping vistas everywhere, altitudes of as much as 14,000 feet in the Rockies. When we topped the small rise, hardwoods yielded for a stretch to conifers. The path was shadowed by the green canopy, carpeted by a layer of fallen needles. On this dank November morning the forest was utterly silent. The earth lay brown and the sky hung suspended with drifting draperies of heavy clouds, layer on layer, light gray, dark gray, sometimes scudding before a surly wind, sometimes masking the landscape in sullen shrouds.

As we dipped again into a hardwood grove, the fallen leaves that a fortnight earlier had spangled the forest floor with gold and scarlet were now faded into the dusty hues of antique murals on crumbling walls. The trunks of the trees channeled tiny rivulets of moisture down to the saturated soil, and from the dark and naked branches no birds called. The migratory birds of summer had departed, and the winter birds—chickadees, nuthatches, pine siskins, jays—had the forest much to themselves. Chipmunks and squirrels, though not yet in their seasonal semihibernation, remained unseen. Suddenly the silence was

Assorted rocks, severed from the side of Wallface Mountain, litter the floor of Indian Pass a few hundred feet south of its highest point.

broken by a most unexpected yammering of mixed voices, arguing, quarreling, interrupting, escalating in volume—a cacophony known to behaviorists as the "cocktail party syndrome." Bob and I looked at each other in astonishment; then suddenly I understood. I looked overhead and saw nothing. But I realized that above the cloud cover an echelon of Canada geese was migrating from northern summer grounds to winter in the south. Far more purposeful than the vocalizing of humans in their cups, the cries of geese in flight are the birds' way of assuring their leader—and one another—that all the members of the formation are present and accounted for. In fog or clouds the cries are uttered more frequently to make up for the lack of visibility.

For the next three miles, the trail continued on its roller-coaster course, up and down, down and up, crossing a series of rivulets that make their way down from McIntyre to Indian Pass Brook. The drizzle occasionally expanded into a brief shower, then expired. The gray light seemed unrelated to calendar or clock. Time and again Bob and I had to detour around low spots in the trail where water had accumulated to a depth of several inches; in these excursions into the bush, we hauled ourselves from sapling to sapling as our feet slithered on the muddy ground. Bob grumbled: "I don't know why anyone wants to live in the East." I refrained from arguing about the relative merits of West and East and explained to this admirer of Western scenery that November is always a wet month in the Adirondacks, and that we were not climbing a mountain but traversing the bottom of a cleft, where liquid runs down from both sides.

Now as we looked about through the mists, we came upon an old fireplace in a grassy meadow known as Scott's Clearing, named for a woodsman who once lived here alone. We picked our way among tall grasses and raspberry bushes and discovered the stony ruins of a dam, built by 19th Century lumbermen to contain a pond beside their camp. No other vestige of the camp remains, save the meadow and the dam, around which the encircling trees are closing in from the renascent forest. At the southwest arc of the clearing, the land drops off to gravel flats on Indian Pass Brook below. We scrambled down a steep bank and forded the brook. Often during fall and spring, rains and beaver swamps render this route impassable, but with a bit of wading we managed to keep on going.

After moving ahead perhaps a hundred yards, we rounded a bend in the brook. There before us, in a stillwater, outlined by sand and gravel flats, we saw a squadron of Canada geese—perhaps the group we had heard a few miles back—refueling in this secret port. They are beautiful creatures with black arched necks, white wimples, salt-and-pepper plumage on wings and body. Bob and I advanced cautiously for a closer look through the rushes and tall grass.

If the geese sensed our presence, they gave no sign. Like tourists at a resort, some were strolling on the beach, some floating lazily in the pool. At this rest stop, they wasted no breath in conversation. Moving very slowly, Bob and I closed the gap to less than 50 feet. I felt certain that the nearest geese could now see us, yet they showed no alarm. However, when we advanced a few feet more, the flight commander pointed his beak straight up at the sky, his neck rigid. The movement, quickly copied in silence by the other geese, was both warning and command. The leader then took to the air. Immediately, the gaggle followed him, and climbed steeply south toward the notch of Indian Pass, falling into precise V-formation. Then, from afar, we heard their voices.

The moment was a lovely one, and it would sustain us during the trials ahead. For now the trail became more demanding. Three times we picked our way across Indian Pass Brook. We walked carefully where we could but sometimes had to leap over round stones too slippery to step on. Small tributary streams descended from either side of the pass. The rain, which had given us a brief respite, returned and Bob moaned, "Why am I here?"

It was almost noon, though without watches we could not have known: there was no sign of the sun in the featureless gray sky. We stood now at the inner portal of Indian Pass. At this point the course of the main stream veers westward, up to its source at Scott Pond, 600 feet above. The pass itself loomed straight ahead, glowering at us. After nearly five miles of muddy but negotiable slopes, we found ourselves looking up with awe at a scene that might have sprung from the fancy of the French artist Gustave Doré, famed as the 19th Century illustrator of Dante's *Inferno*. Nothing I had read about Indian Pass had prepared me for this titanic chaos of rock tumbled from the precipices above. The gorge is indeed nearly vertical. Boulders towered in our path—20, 30 feet high, a frozen pandemonium. The only moving thing within view was a trickle of icy water.

Bob and I halted, wondering whether we could go on; we seemed to be confronted by a cul-de-sac. As the walls closed in, the grade steepened. Meanwhile, the sky darkened as another rain squall approached. We searched for a route along the sides and saw only impassable thickets of dwarf spruce and balsam. We had no alternative but to stay in the bed of the stream, climbing across the wet rocks amid swift rivulets and small falls. From time to time we were forced to scale enormous ledges, fragments of cliff from above.

The uncertainty of our progress ended when we came upon a trail marker directing us to the left, out of the stream bed. Minutes later we reached the divide in the pass, the watershed between the Ausable and Hudson rivers. Although we were standing now on the height of land, we still could not see all of the colossal rock façade of Wallface Mountain, which lay only a few hundred feet to the west, for our view was screened by curtains of evergreen. I knew that in the neighborhood of the pass there was only one promontory from which we could see Wallface entire—Summit Rock, about half a mile south of our present position, and 200 feet lower down. We moved toward Summit Rock, while Bob made me increasingly aware of his disenchantment with the rain, the lack of visibility and, now, pangs of hunger. "You know," he said, "I think this is the lousiest walk I've had since I was in the Army."

But Bob's mood changed when, after another succession of upgrades and downgrades, we found ourselves at the base of Summit Rock, a slanting ledge perhaps 30 feet long and 15 feet wide. This great outcrop stands off to the west of the trail and can easily be missed by any climber who has not been forewarned. It demands a bit of scrambling to reach the top—perhaps 12 feet above the forest floor. Once there, however, you forget everything save what the astonished eye perceives from this high window in the woods. There stands the façade of Wallface: 2,500 feet long, 500 feet high, at first glance unmarred by the weathering of a billion years. But then you begin to discern a few wrinkles of age—small clefts and crannies within which random, wind-blown seeds have alighted and brought forth a feathering of green. These niches in the rockface are the hand- and foot-holds that enable summer rock climbers, roped together above the void, to inch their way up the side of Wallface.

As we looked, no living creature moved on the huge cliff. The summit was shrouded in veils of mist that drifted crazily through the pass, rising and falling with the breath of thermal currents. When we looked down we were able to see the chaos of rock on the floor of the pass, hundreds of feet below, littered with the same geological debris that had blocked our ascent to the height of land and our route to Summit Rock.

For a while, in the drizzle, Bob and I were silent. He appeared stunned by the view, convinced that despite all discomforts the journey had

Partly screened by July foliage, a black bear stands erect to reconnoiter its route. Numerous and shy, Adirondack black bears almost always vanish quickly when humans approach them.

been worthwhile. We opened our knapsacks to find a cold buffet—sandwiches, Coke, beer. As we savored our chilly repast, I gazed down at the chasm and reflected that we were truly in a fastness, the last, lost horizon of the Adirondacks. At this moment, I felt a deep communion with the essence of these mountains. Here, indeed, lay their unique quality: wildness and solitude, surrounded and even intruded upon, in some parts, by civilization. Here in the pass we were completely alone, and felt alone. Today we had encountered no men, no living creatures save the migrant geese.

I downed my cold sandwich, swallowed my cold beer, and momentarily forgot the fitful cold rain. Then a wind joined the party. Where earth and sky had lain quietly together between seamless sheets of gray, their embrace was rudely interrupted by a rush of air, swooping up the pass behind us from the north. It cut the cloud curtain into flapping ribbons of mist that now uncovered the rim of the precipice, now descended about it. For an instant the southern mouth of the pass gaped wide, and we could see the massive spine of Santanoni, 14th tallest, at 4,607 feet, of the High Peaks.

Bob and I looked at each other. It was now after 1 p.m. We had nearly five miles to go before we reached the southern exit of Indian Pass and the first mile of descent from Summit Rock would be as rough and demanding as the climb from the north. We got to our feet, a little stiff from our luncheon break. "Do you realize," I said as we climbed off the rock and started down the trail on the ridge above the gorge, "that every drop of rain that fell on us before lunch will end up in the Saint Lawrence River, and that every raindrop that falls on us now will end up in the Hudson?"

Bob stared at me without answering. Impressed though he was with the view we had just seen, his mind seemed to dwell in cactus country, somewhere in the dry southwest.

After a half mile or so of steep downgrades, with the trail sometimes hacked through thick balsam stands, sometimes narrowing to a perilous, 16-inch-wide catwalk clinging to sheer slopes, we found ourselves on the brink of a ledge, perhaps 20 feet high. We would have been rimrocked had there not been a ladder with wide rungs of spruce, installed by the state. Farther down we came to a similar, second ladder, and after descending it, we executed a tortuous traverse around the base of a 50-foot-high escarpment, deeply cleft, gray-green with lichens, glistening with rivulets.

After that, we faced no more technical mountaineering difficulties. For half a mile we wound through a labyrinth of giant, angular rocks that, like those on the northern approach, are toppled monoliths from the mountain faces above. Soon they were replaced by round boulders, relics of the last ice age, buffed and scoured by rain and running water. The boulders in turn became small cobbles; the cobbles turned to pebbles as we arrived at the left bank of the embryonic Hudson River. At this point the Hudson is a stream barely 10 feet wide, which we crossed on a bridge of two logs wired together. Then the trail rises gently, wandering above the creek bed and following easy contours as the pass widens to east and west.

However, at a low place where three rivulets descend to join Indian Pass Brook, the ground became so boggy that we had to haul our boots out of the muck with every step. Though Bob had ceased to complain, I began to feel some concern about the trail's condition, which was the result not just of rain and rivulets, but of overuse by humans. For even though the Park Agency has waged and won campaigns to protect the wilderness from motorized vehicles—Jeeps, motorboats, snowmobiles, and float planes all having been barred from substantial parts of the state forest preserve—the humble hiker has now joined the ranks of ecological despoilers. Our boots, like those of all the hikers who had preceded us, were tearing into this trail, contributing to its slow breakdown. Similarly, the trail up Marcy from Heart Lake has gradually sunk below the surrounding terrain, tramped down by hundreds of thousands of wilderness walkers, and has since been eroded by rains and spring runoffs so that it appears, in some places, more a stream bed than a footpath. There are, unfortunately, dozens of other examples throughout the Adirondacks.

Perhaps most disturbing to botanists and ecologists is the widespread destruction of fragile plant communities on the higher summits. As George D. Davis of the Adirondack Park Agency has observed: "The alpine areas are traversed by so many hikers that the plants unique to this zone are being ground into the soil. . . . Vegetation, protected as a state resource, is being trampled to death by those for whom it has been protected." And Robert F. Hall, editor of *The Conservationist,* writing of trail erosion and the increasing problem of trash and litter at campsites, inquired in a recent editorial: "How long can the satisfaction of wilderness solitude exist if the use and overuse of the hiking trails, canoe routes and campsites continue to grow at the rate of five

In this view from Summit Rock (foreground), the flank of Wallface Mountain plunges sheer into the depths of Indian Pass.

to ten per cent a year? This has already raised in some minds the need for a permit system to limit visitors in certain fragile areas."

As we slogged down the trail, I told Bob about the proposal. He exploded: "Permit system! A permit to go into the woods! That's destroying our liberty!" I asked him if he had any other suggestions. He hesitated, and I told him that the only alternatives I had heard discussed were re-routing the trails or closing down the lean-tos and hostels. Both are unlikely.

Silence again. The sky lightened somewhat. The rain tapered off. But my mind remained on environmental battles, lost and won, and problems that lie ahead. The original creation of the Adirondack Park Agency in 1971; the approval in 1972 of the State Land Master Plan for the Adirondacks, which divided the area into wilderness and other categories; and the adoption in 1973 of the Land Use and Development Plan regulating private lands were all battles won—but not total victories. Both Davis and Hall agree that these successes should not inspire complacency. "The shoreline restrictions in the regulations are grossly inadequate," Davis points out. "They essentially allow, and even encourage, encircling the park's accessible lakes and ponds with buildings. This limits the enjoyment of water to a few landowners. It can also threaten the quality of the water."

It was 5 p.m. and twilight crept through the November woods. The trail had taken us onto an old logging road. We glimpsed Henderson Lake on our right and soon we were at the parking lot where we had left our second car. Gratefully, we got in and drove south past the ghost town of Adirondac, past the ancient McIntyre blast furnace, still standing. On our left, the young Hudson, here 20 feet wide, rushed noisily over boulders, small falls and rifts.

As we approached the great scar of the titanium mine, a company guard stepped onto the road and ordered us to halt. We heard a siren and an unintelligible voice over a speaker system.

"What's going on?" I asked.

"You'll have to stop here a few minutes," the guard said politely. "They're going to blast."

I thought that this was a terrible way to end a day in the wilderness, sitting waiting for an explosion. The moment arrived: a muffled roar reverberated from the unseen heights of Marcy. As I watched, tumbling clouds of smoke and dust appeared. Flying rock fragments soared into the air, silhouetted against the sky. Some fell not far from where we stood, some splashed into the waters of the river. At this point, I mused, the Hudson loses its virginity.

I was depressed by the incident. Then, somewhat reluctantly, I faced the fact that the miners had despoiled only a few acres out of the six million in the Adirondack Park. And I recalled that the dedicated people working against further damage to the park are currently optimistic —though still guarded and alert. My spirits rose further when I remembered a conversation a few weeks earlier with Richard W. Lawrence Jr., chairman of the Adirondack Park Agency. Despite the threats represented by industrial and recreational pressures, Lawrence believes very strongly in the compatibility of people with the Adirondacks. He sees not paradox, but accord.

"Do you realize," he said, "that the Adirondack Park is just about the only place in the whole nation where people can live in a *park*? There are some private holdings in a few parks, but you can't actually *live* in the Yellowstone, Yosemite, Glacier or Olympic parks. You can visit and camp, but not reside in them. That's why I think the idea of private land inside this park is such a marvelous one. As a matter of fact, I think the whole United States should be a park.

"But this great concept—the mixture of state land and private land —presents an enormous challenge. For what we have to do is preserve the park environment. A false issue has grown up—an issue that looks upon people and the environment as adversaries. The implication is that if environment takes priority, people will somehow be deprived. That's nonsense. It's possible to have both."

The Ponds of Autumn

PHOTOGRAPHS BY JOHN CHANG McCURDY

Autumn does not sweep into the Adirondacks in a sudden onset as it sometimes does in New England with tartans of gold and red swarming in a single day along the hills and through the valleys. Autumn advances slowly, sending scouts and harbingers ahead into the fading country of summer. It is on the Adirondack ponds or beside them that a photographer can best record the slow, silent invasion.

Mist rises from the ponds; the surface of the water, lately bright as silver, begins to turn as dark as lead. A tiny noise breaks the quietness and the photographer, wheeling, sees a ring of ripples spreading where a solitary leaf has fallen.

Something unseen glides over the still-green grasses beside the ponds and bends them down. The grasses remain bent, as though hunched against snow and sleet gathering beyond the horizon half a world away. The sun is low, losing its heat. It peers slantwise through the trees. Yet its light, striking through a few translucent leaves on black boughs above the water, makes them gleam like freshly minted gold coins.

The gray vapor keeps issuing from the ponds; from these, which are deliberately left nameless here, and from thousands of other ponds scattered among the mountains, the mist drifts upward. In the deepening haze the ponds are touched with mystery. An old name for them that suggests dark depths and strangeness comes out of the past into the mind: tarns.

A rounded gray rock rises out of the water. Warmed all the long summer by the sun, now it is losing its heat and soon it will be as cold as fog compressed into solid form. Beside another pond white birches stand as proudly as they did in May, but the outriders of autumn have already brushed past them. In spring the leaves of birches caught the eye; now it is the woody skeletons on which they hang.

Some of the trees beside the ponds remain green and apparently untouched. But in the night an autumn soldier moves soundlessly among them; dawn reveals a single stricken maple turned red as blood.

The tiny, almost inaudible sound comes again—perhaps a fish rising, a bubble coming up from the ooze below, another leaf falling, or perhaps something else. The photographer turns once more to watch the circle of quiet ripples widening across the dark pond, fading as the season fades, silent on the water.

WATER: RIPPLES AND REFLECTION

WIND-BENT GRASS